Trojan Church:
The New Age Corruption
Of The
Evangelical Faith

Dr. Gregory R Reid

PRESS

Trojan Church:
The New Age Corruption Of The Evangelical Faith
by Dr. Gregory R Reid

Printed in the United States of America

ISBN 978-1-60647-733-5

www.xulonpress.com

A Forward Thought

—〰—

Writing this book has been one of the most difficult tasks I have ever undertaken. I have prayed and agonized over everything that I have written. At one point I asked God for a word of comfort about it all. I opened my Bible in church right after that prayer, and this is what He gave me: "Do not diminish a word." (Jeremiah 26:2b)

I am aware that the spirit of the prophet is subject to the prophet. Though I am no prophet, I realize the way I have written is in some measure a product of the person God made me to be. However, part of not diminishing a word is not going back over what I have written to make sure I have not offended people. This *will* offend people. But I believe God is offended at the way this generation has been hijacked by people with best selling books and good marketing plans who are leading people down a fruitless if not destructive, and most definitely unbiblical path.

In some ways, the urgency of this book has caused me to write unedited. It is not written from a scholarly perspective, but from the perspective of a search and rescue spiritual paramedic. I see the spiritual savaging of the church and especially this generation and I do not have time to waste having a "conversation" about these things. I want to see at least a good portion of this generation saved, equipped, and given the power to stand strong in Jesus no matter what the cost. There is no time for niceties.

I can't defend myself against critics who will attack the polemic style of this writing, or criticize its lack of scholarliness. Frankly, I am just an old war dog, not a theologian. But I am extremely jealous over God's Word, and I will oppose any attempt to minimize the Word of God and lead this generation into spiritual ruination by tampering with the scriptures. (See Revelation 22:18 for a sneak preview of what is awaiting those who do so.)

I have written this in hopes of waking up my own generation to return to the truth we have abandoned. I have also written in the hopes of helping raise up a young generation of Truth Bearers that will go to war for the souls of this world who do not know Jesus Christ. I can only pray that they will hear me.

You do not go into a life and death crisis speaking smooth words. You go in determined to save lives. That is what I have tried to do. I have done it with a heart that is ablaze to pull back the massive veil of blinding deception that has taken over much of the Western church and proclaim the truth loud enough to be heard over the anesthetizing voice of the enemy that is cooing, "Peace, peace," when there is no peace.

In the words of Einstein, if you are out to describe the truth, leave elegance to the tailor.

My prayer is that I have succeeded in doing the former, for I have surely done the latter. May God use these words to speak clarity into the hearts that can hear what the Spirit of the Lord is saying to the church in this hour.

Acknowledgements

—ɷ—

I am deeply indebted to those who have provided their insights, knowledge and resources concerning the issues I have written of in this book. Thanks to Johanna Michaelsen for the pioneer work she has done and still does in a very difficult field where there are very few who are left guarding the gates of the house of God. Thanks to Deborah and Lighthouse Trails, whose resources are unmatched.

I dedicate this book to the Sox crew. Thanks for being such a major part of my life, for listening to my long rants about these things and especially for giving me hope for the future of the church. You are the warriors I have longed to see on the battlefield. Go tear it up for Jesus and never look back. I'll be on the battle line cheering you on.

Finally, to "The Fellowship" – the Maranatha brothers. Though the fellowship has broken, wherever we go, I will carry a part of you with me. "And in dreams, we will meet again."

Gregory R Reid

"This will be written for the generation to come." Psalm 102:18

"The truth is a lighted stronghold.
We must dwell therein or perish."

Amy Carmichael

I Had A Dream...

—∿∿—

There were kids gathered together to worship on a hillside. They were in love with Jesus, and worshipping with all their hearts as an older worship leader led them from a stage.

I heard a loud voice yelling from behind the stage. I went back to see what it was. A garish, obnoxious preacher who looked like a carnival barker was preaching to a crowd with great passion. He held up a banner that had symbols for Hinduism, Islam, a cross, a Star of David, and every great world religion in a circle surrounding these words: "One World, One Religion." "THIS is the future church!" the man screamed, and as chills overcame me, I ran back to the young people. "This is it," I shouted. "Jesus is coming back!" The sky turned black; we all fell to our knees and worshipped. The end had come.

I had dreamed of what would soon come. Even now, the FutureChurch is being built.

That is why this book was written, so you know, and are warned, and will stay faithful to the truth to the end.

History of the FutureChurch

—♏︎—

In the not too distant future, the church will undergo a trans-formation that will change its heart and soul and foundation completely.

The FutureChurch is the deliberately designed dream of those moving the world toward globalism, "One World – One Religion."

Two or three decades ago, the obstacles to such a transforma-tion were so many as to make the task almost impossible. But, said the tortoise to the hare, slow and steady wins the race. And while the church has run hare-like into trends, megachurch programs and media-driven movements, the New Age tortoise has come into the back door and planted within our walls the tares of deception and illusion that are transforming the church into a New Age apparatus and puppet from *within*.

Did God Really Say...?

—ɯ—

In the garden, Satan's ploy was "Did God really say...?" It is still his strongest weapon: He is always getting people to question God's truth, His will, His love, and His intentions for His children.

In his confrontation with Jesus in the wilderness, it was the same ploy, with more theological flourishes: "Didn't God say His angels would bear you up on their wings, lest you dash your foot on a stone? Go ahead and throw yourself down from here and prove it..." Now he'd gone to quoting scripture to get his way, to get Jesus to do things Satan's way – the satanic way – the way of self-will, self-wisdom, self-pride.

Jesus simply quoted the Word of God. And when Satan quoted scripture and said, "God said," Jesus struck back with, "But it is also written..." Jesus fought against well-crafted and even "scripturally based" lies with further truth from the scriptures revealing Satan's lies for what they were – *partial truths meant to deceive.*

Satan's ploy remains the same. He's still out to get people to question truth, question God, question the Bible. That's why you hear a lot about "rethinking" and "reframing" and "we need a new vocabulary." Satan wants to distort, change, and repackage truth, twisted just enough to alter the power of truth but not enough to show his hand as the one who did it.

The answer to the Satanic altering of truth that is working through contemplative prayer, Purpose-Driven, Seeker-Friendly and Emergent Church distortions, misuse and deletions of scripture is to say, "Thus says the Word of the Lord," "What says the Word of the Lord?" and "It is written, and *again* it is written." Though they may mock and denigrate the idea of living only according to the truth of the Word of God – "Sola Scriptura" – which means, "only scripture" - it works, and has worked since the beginning of time and always will. We move off of that mark to our own destruction.

The Face of the FutureChurch

—ɯ—

It will be Wordless.
It will be spineless.

It will be sentimental like an old drunk and as vulnerable as a wandering child.

It will have no view of heaven, or spiritual warfare, or Jesus' return.

It will be handing out cookies and hoping the world will be nicer to them and be friends on the global playground.

It will be as clueless as Scarlett saying, "I'll think about that tomorrow!" and as bright and cheery as Little Orphan Annie singing, "Tomorrow, tomorrow, I love ya, tomorrow!"

And, as Jesus said, they knew not until the flood came and took them all away.

For when *that* tomorrow comes, their New Age fantasy will disappear.

And they will face the Lamb and the Lion,

And there will be weeping and gnashing of teeth as they meet a Jesus they never really knew.

Everything Will Change

—∞—

Christ-consciousness and Christ-abilities are the natural inheritance of every human being on Earth. When the word of this hope has reached the nations, the end of this phase of evolution shall come. All will know their choice. All will be required to choose.... All who choose not to evolve will die off.[1]

Barbara Marx Hubbard, New Age leader and author of *The Revelation*, from *Happy Birth Day, Planet Earth.*

If your church has been plateaued for six months, it might take six months to get it going again. If it's been plateaued a year, it might take a year. If it's been plateaued for 20 years, you've got to set in for the duration! I'm saying some people are going to have to die or leave. Moses had to wander around the desert for 40 years while God killed off a million people before he let them go into the Promised Land. That may be brutally blunt, but it's true. There may be people in your church who love God sincerely, but who will never, ever change. [2]

Rick Warren, Pastors.Com

Reinvent yourself for the 21st century or die. Some would rather die than change. [3]

Leonard Sweet, Emergent Church leader, *Soul Tsunami*, Pp. 17, 75

Evolve or die. [4]

Eckhart Tolle, New Age writer, *A New Earth*, Pp. 21-22

The Blueprint

—ᴍ—

In order for One World and One Religion to come to reality, there is a clear blueprint for dismantling the evangelical church and making it part of the coming FutureChurch. As you read this book, this blueprint will become increasingly obvious as you recognize how it is being implemented in nearly every sector of the church:

1. Tear down the integrity and importance of the Word of God
2. Promote church growth as a mass marketing plan and not a Spirit-birthed event
3. Introduce Hindu and Buddhist meditation and prayer styles
4. Make other religions appear to be compatible with Christianity
5. Substitute the power of God to change lives with a social gospel that will make the church a relief agency
6. Eliminate the prophetic
7. Change the language of the church to make it compatible with the New Age and all religions
8. Introduce signs and lying wonders and false supernatural manifestations

Once these specific details of this blueprint become clear to you, you will begin to see it in nearly every corner of our modern church world. Once the language of the new age becomes familiar to you, you will begin to see how thoroughly the modern church has adopted it.

Chapter One

Once Upon A Time...

—ɱ—

Lucifer – "light bearer" – wanted to be God. He wrote in blazing words in rebellion across the heavens, "I WILL!"

He was cast out of heaven to earth, he and his angelic brethren who rebelled with him, to earth. He then began his campaign to overthrow God and regain his glory by seducing our First Parents, Adam and Eve. "God knows," he told them, "that the minute you eat of the fruit, your eyes will be opened, and you will be as gods, knowing good and evil." (Gen. 3:5) They bit. But rather than obtain godhood, they began to die. Sin – the fatal disease of Satan's kin – was now in our blood.

But God provided a sacrifice – a blood sacrifice - since only blood can atone for sin. "You will bruise His heel," he told the Evil One. "But He (the Messiah) will crush your head." It was the First Prophecy of many leading to His coming, His Death, resurrection and return.

But Satan (ex-Lucifer) never lost his insane hatred for God and for Jesus, and he continued his campaign for Godhood. But what is a god without a following? He had no place beyond the earth and its skies to rule – so here he would carry out his grand scheme. He knew he would not reclaim the position in heaven with God that he once enjoyed. But he WOULD be "prince of this world" (John 14:30) and mislead the creatures God so loved into ruin and despair, and eventually, damnation.

He would demand worship, for he needed it.

He created false gods. He could not show his real face or nature, for he is "a liar and the father of it." (John 8:44). So he created images and false gods – Chemosh, Baal, Ashtoreth, Moloch - and people served, and prostituted themselves, and defiled themselves, and sacrificed the innocent on their altars, while the Evil One breathed in the power from all they gave him, without them ever knowing he was the REAL power behind their vile worship.

His religion would be based on his original sin – self-worship, self-serving, and self-will – "I will be as God." He drove man to build into the heavens (the tower of Babel), divine the future (astrology), and open themselves to hoards of demons and fallen angels (necromancy, séances, Ouija boards and other forms of divination) so that one by one, people would become the "vehicles" by which they – HE – would rule, if not OVER heaven, then at least under it, out from under its rule, for man will have given him reign over a godless world.

Time and again he attempted his coup d'état – through kings and rulers, through Nero and Nebuchadnezzar and Hitler, Mao and Stalin, and each time, God's chosen survived and the Standard of Truth and the work of the Gospel remained. Each time, the church thrived in persecution and grew.

Despite the setbacks, Satan's plan has never stopped being implemented on every level.

Over a century ago, the plan took a written form, most notably through a Russian Occultist named Madame Helena Petrovna Blavatsky (1831-1891). The foundational theology for the occult and New Age world were written down by her in her two books, *Isis Unveiled* and *The Secret Doctrine*, as well as through the magazine she founded in September, 1887, *Lucifer*, a monthly magazine designed, as stated on its title page, "to bring to light the hidden things of darkness." Blavatsky put forth the teaching of the "Ascended Masters" and the Root Races – races she claimed explained each era of man – the Polarian, Hyperborean, Lemurian, Atlantean, and during her time, the *Aryan*. (Alice Bailey, the spiritual heir-apparent to Theosophy, further elucidated the Luciferian doctrines that would later be the grid for the modern New Age movement).

A young man later took these teachings very much to heart. The result was the Third Reich and the slaughter of millions of Jews and others under the demonic hand of a trained occult master named Adolph Hitler. The "Ascended Masters" (in Christian and Jewish theology, the fallen angels) had their first New World taste of world dominance.

It was the perfect picture of Lucifer's New Age religion's "end game" when it was allowed free reign.

Fast forward to the 1960's: It was the dawning of the Age of Aquarius. The "Ascended Masters" had succeeded in turning much of the Western church into a powerless social club, with the exception of strong moves of God within some denominations, on the mission field, in revivals, and especially through the Jesus Movement. A whole generation of restless, unhappy youth was ready for the "initiation."

Lucifer used the age-old formula – for the Greeks, Dionysus, (god of wine); Aphrodite, (goddess of love); and the Muses (gods of music, art and poetry.) In the roaring twenties, it became wine, women and song, and in the 60's, sex, drugs and rock 'n' roll. It blew a psychic hole so wide into the youth culture that the Doors of Perception would alter forever, the Age of Aquarius would come to full day, Satanist Aleister Crowley's pronouncement that "Everybody is a Star" would become an anthem by Sly and the Family Stone, and that 60's generation, and the ones to follow, would be thrust into a world where occultism and Paganism and sorcery (in Greek, "pharmakia" – drug taker) would be accepted and desired.

Many players stepped onto the stage to provide meaning, cohesion and direction to this "brave new world" of mystic spirituality and drug induced occult experiences. Most notable have been Marilyn Ferguson (author of *The Aquarian Conspiracy*), Barbara Marx Hubbard (author of *The Revelation*), Marianne Williamson, (author of *A Return to Love* and a recent favorite New Age teacher of Oprah Winfrey), Neale Donald Walsch (author of the *Conversations With God* books, which absolves Hitler of guilt for slaughtering millions of Jews. Examples of "God" talking to him: "Hitler went to heaven."[1] "Because Hitler did nothing wrong. Hitler simply did what he did."[2] "The mistakes Hitler made did no harm or damage to those whose deaths he caused. Those souls were released from their earthly bondage. . . . No one who has experienced death *ever mourns the death of anyone.*"[3] Other recent New Age proponents include well-known authors Deepak Chopra and Wayne Dyer, Esther Hicks (*The Secret*'s "trance channeler" for the "Abraham Group" that spoke through her to give us that book, recently made famous by Rhonda Byrne) and Eckhard Tolle (author of *A New Earth* and *The Power of Now*).

Most Christians have never heard of these people. Yet they are some of the architects of the Future Church and much of what we are seeing take shape in the Purpose-Driven, Seeker-Friendly and Emergent Church movement. They, along with the most powerful and influential media spokesperson for and promoter of the New Age religion, Oprah Winfrey, have laid out a theology, a doctrine and a future plan so clear, concise in its *uniformity* and *conformity* to the coming One World/One Religion template that it is breathtaking. It is a future that does not propose to *eliminate* the church, but to slowly *transform* it. Many churches that for many years have not held to Biblical principles and fundamental truth in the Word of God have been in the loop of the New Age Church to come for some time. The only ones left to deal with were the evangelical churches – the ones who *did* believe in the infallible Word of God, the second coming of Jesus, the tribulation and last days, Jesus as the only way to the Father, and other bedrock Christian doctrines. They have to slowly absorb this part of the church, change it, one tiny thing at a time, one doctrine and one pillar and one truth at a time, until it will be barely recognizable as what was once the stalwart steward of Jesus' Gospel. It will instead become a lost, helpless and powerless lapdog that the "One World religion" will easily absorb and use as a harmless spiritual village idiot that will hand out sandwiches to the poor to prove its usefulness in the postmodern age.

In the 1980's, the *new* New Age – the evolutionary brainchild of Blavatsky, Bailey and Ferguson – was in full bloom. Hindu meditation, which had snuck into the schools under the scientific sounding principles expounded as TM (Transcendental Meditation) was fast gaining educational sanction and sainthood. Children's cartoons, movies and books were jam-packed with heavy occult themes and symbols borrowed from Wicca, Paganism, Hinduism, Buddhism and even black magick. A whole generation was being conditioned and acclimated to accept occultic things as normal and harmless, or worse, unrecognized and undetected.

Actress Shirley MacLaine became the first prophetess of the modern New Age, risking career and respect to preach her newfound religion of karma, reincarnation, crystals and a New World Religion.

The evangelical church was busy building Mega Media Ministries and becoming a political animal – too busy to notice all of this - until two brave women wrote books that exposed the *real* New Age agenda. Constance Cumbey wrote *The Hidden Dangers of the Rainbow,* and Johanna Michaelsen wrote *Lambs to the Slaughter.*

Because of their efforts, many believers woke up and started to warn others. They realized that when well-known New Age leader Benjamin Crème took out a full page ad in the Wall Street Journal proclaiming, "The Christ is Now Here" and announcing that "Lord Maitreya" was in London and would soon manifest himself and bring world peace, that New Agers were not just people we could write off derogatorily as "flaky tree-hugging crystal gazers." They were wealthy, powerful people like Crème, Mikhail Gorbachev and a host of other world players and financial movers and shakers who all believed in a One World government and a coming Man of Peace. Many believers began to realize that Jesus' prophecy that "Many shall come in My Name and say I am the Christ" was being fulfilled.

After a fairly concerted and very successful effort to silence the messengers who warned of the New Age, the *public* face of the New Age largely dropped out of sight but the force behind the New Age continued its works through world political and social events while continuing the media desensitizing and conditioning.

And on this side of the ring, we now have a whole new generation of Christians who do not have a clue about what the New Age is, have been raised compromised on the occult through the media and ten years of Harry Potter, and is ripe for the picking.

The Now Children. The Quantum Leap Generation. The Star Children. The Indigo Children.

The FutureChurch.

What's new is very old, indeed.

The names and players have changed, from New Age to "Emergent" and "Postmodern" – from Blavatsky and Bailey to Marianne Williamson and Robert Schuller and Rob Bell and Brian McLaren – but the *agenda* proceeds at a brisk pace toward the fulfillment of Daniel and Revelation and all things End Times.

It is an agenda orchestrated by Lucifer himself through his fallen hordes and his human agents and mouthpieces. It is a plan not just for One World and one rule but to create one hideous Frankenstein religion stitched together with thread of occult material, stitched together from them *all* – One World, one religion, and "One lord to rule them all." He is the one who still craves worship and will, according to scripture, possess a human vessel and in a time of world crisis like the world has never seen, come as a "man of peace." Neale Donald Walsch, New Age writer of the *Conversation With God* books, first put forth a "PEACE Plan" and within a short time, Rick Warren *also* came out with a "P.E.A.C.E. Plan,"[4] slightly different from Walsh's, but also moving steadily along "on the same page" with many New Age ideals and agendas – world peace, curing disease, feeding the poor. These "peace plans" await the "Man of Peace." In fact Rick Warren has said he always goes into a village looking for "the man of peace." Rick Warren says:

> **Who's the man of peace in any village - or it might be a woman of peace - who has the most respect, they're open and they're influential? They don't have to be a Christian. In fact, they could be a Muslim, but they're open and they're influential and you work with them to attack the five giants. And that's going to bring the second Reformation.**[5] [Not the second coming of Jesus – g.r.]

But the scriptures are *so* clear: "When they say peace and safety, then sudden destruction will come upon them." (2 Thessalonians 5:3) The man of peace *will* come – not the Prince of Peace who said He would come in the clouds where *every eye would see Him* – but he will come - Satan come in the flesh - promoted as the reincarnation of Krishna, the Fifth Buddha, the Imam Madhi of Islam, the Messiah of the Jews and the Christ of the church.

There was a time I could not imagine that *anyone* who read the scriptures could fall for these lies. But now, in this first dawning of the new millennium, I can actually see that before it is over, much of the evangelical church will actually believe that they have misinterpreted all the prophecies concerning the coming of Jesus so that when this "Man of Peace" comes, pastors worldwide will have been so deluded that they will proclaim, "We were wrong about what we thought the Bible said about how Jesus will return. He *has* returned – and He is here now!" If you do not believe that, you have no idea how deeply infected with New Age deception and lies the church already is.

The evangelical church has been a huge block to the devil and his plans for a One World government and religion under his rule – and to the architects of the New Age - until now. For within the last few decades, Satan and his hordes and human puppets have chipped away at the wall of truth, injected hedonistic pleasures and prosperity, told well-crafted and beautiful lies, taken out discernment and sown the tares of destructive occultism so thoroughly that now, all they must do is water them – and wait. They will grow. They *are* growing and in this decade, they are beginning to bear poisoned fruit. It is the fruit of the original lie. "Did God really say...didn't we misunderstand the scriptures...does the Bible really say that... take a bite..."

Jesus said, if possible, even the elect would be deceived. (Mark 13:22) The scriptures warn that there will be a strong delusion, and doctrines of devils, and seducing spirits. Can't you see it? Don't you know we are possibly on the cusp of the Great Apostasy to end them *all*?

Is that hard for you to believe?

Then please allow me to show you the clear blueprint of the enemy, as simply as I can, and let you decide what is true, and what to do. If you decide to open your eyes and act, it may cost you dearly.

Because you see, there is a "selection process" coming for religious dissenters, for those who are "fundamentalists," "haters," "apocalyptic anarchists," believers in the tribulation to come, "narrow minded religious bigots" and "Bible thumpers." You will begin to be, perhaps even in your own Purpose-Driven/Seeker-Friendly/ Emergent Church fellowship, marginalized, tagged as a divisive person and others will be told to "mark those who cause division among you and have nothing to do with them." Your concerns about the influx of New Age influence and teaching in the church will at first be tolerated, then noted, and finally, threatened into silence.

If you hold to the unchangeable truth of the Word of God and insist that it be the standard for the church of Jesus Christ, prepare to be mocked, ridiculed, cartooned, and patronized. Speak of these truths and you are not likely to make many friends. But for those desiring to contend for the faith of Jesus and the truth of His Word that millions have spilled their blood for, silence is *not* an option.

We must speak, because it is right to do so. It is, admittedly, easier not to. It is becoming as difficult as Salmon swimming upstream to speak of truth and Biblical absolutes. We are witnessing the Lemming Generation – helpless, frantic, and willing to jump off the cliff with the head lemming simply because he's in the lead, and well, there are multitudes of others going that way too, so how can it be wrong? We cannot withhold the truth of the Word of God, no matter how popular, how famous or how accepted those who are teaching contrary to it are.

This book has been written in the belief that God is going to wake up an army of believers that refuse to go with the crowd of trendy truths and convenient Christianity and that will not bow the knee to the infected and poisonous theology that is now pouring into the church almost without restraint. I commit the truths of this book to them in trust that the true church will rise up out of the mud of this spiritual morass called the "Postmodern Church." May you be strengthened – and equipped – to resist this absorbing of the church of Jesus Christ into the mutated monster FutureChurch.

Chapter Two

The Occult, the New Age and the Emergent Church: Understanding the Basics

—ᵐ—

In our modern church world that has gone almost two decades without any substantial teaching about the dangers of the occult and the New Age, we have left ourselves and our youth exceptionally vulnerable to all manner of deception, occult practices disguised in religious garments, and New Age socialization and globalization dressed as "doing church." If we have any hope of stemming the tide of the massive wave of spiritual darkness that has come as an angel of light to cripple the church, we have to first have at least a base understanding of (1) What the occult is, (2) What the New Age is, (3) What the Emergent Church is, and (4) The terminology, language and buzzwords that these groups use. This is by no means an exhaustive study, but will at least give you a "sense of the thing" and will train your spirit to recognize the Deceiver when he comes – however he comes.

What Is The Occult?

The word "occult" means "hidden". Essentially, the occult is a broad range of activities, practices and philosophies which include:

Tarot cards, Ouija boards, palm reading, psychics, consulting with mediums, séances and communication with the dead (necromancy), astrology, mind reading, mind control, astral projection (leaving your body), I Ching, fortune telling, witchcraft, Wicca, white magick, black magick, Satanism, Vampyrism, sorcery, wizardry, spells and spellwork, curandismo, voodoo, Santeria, Yoga, transcendental meditation, reincarnation, past life regression, Kabbalah, Buddhism, Hinduism.

No Christian under any circumstances should be involved in any of these activities or believe any of these philosophies. They are scripturally forbidden by God. If you are, you need to stop, repent, and throw away everything related to it – books, jewelry, statues, artwork, anything. God forbids it all.

What Is The New Age?

The New Age and the New Age Movement are broad terms describing a wide variety of groups, activities, ideology, theology, practices and terminology. The birth and development of the New Age movement goes back centuries and has gradually unfolded from some of the original concepts put forth by Helena Petrovna Blavatsky, mother of Luciferian based Theosophy and her successor Alice Bailey, who published Lucifer's Trust (later to become Lucis Trust, still an existing organization with ties to the U.N.), the Golden Dawn and other esoteric and/or occult based groups into what it is today. The New Age and the occult are essentially one and the same. What was once "hidden" is now open for all.

Some of the activities, groups, philosophies and practices of the New Age include:

Guided visualization, self-actualization, self-realization, self-awareness, crystal magick, crystal healing, UFOlogy, Global Peace Groups, TM, (transcendental meditation), Yoga, trance-channeling, spirit guides, Ascended Masters, Wise Ones, Ancient Ones, psychic reading, past life regression, aura reading and kirlian or aura photography, EST, Scientology, Dianetics, group meditations, tantric sex, kundalini Yoga, some forms of massage therapy (especially Reiki) and so on.

Some major voices in the New Age movement are: Marianne Williamson, author of *A Return to Love*; Neale Donald Walsch, author of the *Conversations with God* books; Barbara Marx Hubbard, author of *The Revelation*; Jack Canfield and Mark Victor Hansen, authors of the wildly successful *Chicken Soup For The Soul* series; Benjamin Crème, forerunner for "Maitreya"; Oprah Winfrey, the media central go-to person for all things New Age; Esther Hicks, who trance-channeled the "Abraham Group" whose "message" became the basis for the book and DVD *The Secret* by Rhonda Byrne, also a major New Age voice; Eckhart Tolle, author of *A New Earth* and many others, too numerous to name.

The dream of the New Age Luciferian order, as previously stated, followed a progression of teachings and books beginning with Helena Blavatsky, then Alice Bailey. From there a whole host of people took up this mantle, including Marilyn Ferguson (author of *The Aquarian Conspiracy*) Shirley MacLaine and various Hollywood luminaries who are following the path of "enlightenment" via the New Age Movement.

In the last few decades, the New Age has come into full blossom and become part of much of our culture, media and education. If there is a common agenda, it is for One World, one religion, global peace, and realizing man's Divinity. It is heavily invested in the Green movement, animal rights groups, and radical feminist groups. It is tolerant of all faiths, except one – Biblical Christianity. One is free to believe anything one wishes, so long as one does not believe that the Bible is the only truth and the infallible, inspired Word of God and that Jesus is the only way to salvation.

Here are a few of the terms, "buzzwords" if you will, that are prevalent with New Agers and the New Age movement, and can help to recognize when a person, group or teaching may be of New Age derivation:

Actualize, actualization, aligning, alignment, at-one-ment, be still, center, centering, change agent, (the) Christ spirit, Christ consciousness, coach, common ground, consciousness shift, contemplative, convergence, consensus, consensus building, deconstruction, destiny, dialogue, dialoguing, diverse, diversity, divine, (the) divine within, doomsday, doomsday preaching, doomsday theology, dream, finding your dream, fulfilling your dream, force, forces (as relates to the "divine" or God), God's Dream, dare to dream, empowering, emerging, emergent, enlightenment, evolutionary, evolutionary shift, finding your center, getting aligned with God, getting centered, Global, global shift, Global Village, God is in all things (panentheism), guided visualization, imagine, imagination, imagining, inclusive, intentions, lone ranger, mystical, new reformation, on the same page, paradigm, planetary, Planetary Pentecost, quantum leap, quantum shift, reimagining, reframing, relational, rethinking, self-realization, self-actualization, send a message, shift, soul force, source, step up to the plate, team player, The One, transformation, transformative, transitioning, tolerance, transcendent, transcendence, unity-in-diversity, universe, universal reality, ultimate reality, vision, vision casting, vision quest or questing, visualize, visualizing, world peace, World Citizen, World Servers, etc.

There are a growing number of Christians who are making frequent use of these terms without knowing where they come from or what they mean in the New Age or occult world. Even though some of these words have innocent usage in a Christian framework, most of them are in fact rooted in New Age and occult teachings and philosophies, and are in clear opposition to Biblical truth. A word like "transformation" for a believer is a Biblical one, based on scriptural principles: i.e., "Be transformed by the renewing of your mind." But the New Age meaning of "transformative" and "transformational" is about a cosmic shift in thinking in order to reach the "divine within." So a New Ager could use the word, and it would cause no alarm with a believer unless we understood the intent. Other words, such as "vision casting" is a clear occult concept having to do with magick and spellwork. It was simply injected into the Christian world with a different meaning; but the BASIS of that phrase is rooted in the occult. Knowing that there may be innocent usage of these New Age terms and many who do not understand their original meaning, this is my own rule of thumb:

Using a few words that may be found in the New Age vocabulary is almost inevitable because it has become part of our cultural and social vocabulary.

Using five or more on a consistent basis is a leaning.

Over ten as part of someone's teaching structure is a belief system, and its users need to be either educated and corrected – or, should it become evident that they are actually involved willfully in New Age doctrine and activities - exposed.

What is the Emergent Church?

Out of nowhere it seems, in the last decade, the Emergent Church has become a major movement in the evangelical West. It is difficult to precisely define, but one thing is becoming fairly certain: it is becoming a breeding ground for nearly every New Age concept, teaching and practice there is or has been in the history of the church. Although it is difficult to give a completely accurate description of the Emergent Church, because of the wide range of voices and people who are in it, the following is a rough description based on the current literature and leaning of those who consider themselves Emergent:

- Scripture is no longer the ultimate authority for many well-known "Emergent Church" leaders. They rely heavily on new and exotic Bible "translations" and "paraphrases" such as *The Message*.

- Emergent thought leans increasingly, and heavily, on contemplative prayer concepts that closely mirror eastern occult meditation techniques, as well as labyrinths, guided visualization, etc. The result is a moving away from evangelism and the true work of the Gospel and toward esoteric practices like inner silence, breath prayers and eastern-style meditation.

- The Gospel of Jesus is being replaced with "serving the world" activities and methods that promote church growth and a social gospel at the expense of making true disciples through the teaching and preaching of the Word of God and reaching a lost humanity for Jesus.

- Emphasis on the "here and now," fixing your life, and little or no emphasis on the return of Jesus and of coming judgment.

- Increasing emphasis on "repairing the world" and establishing the "kingdom now" rather than expecting judgment and Jesus' return, the creating of a new heaven and a new earth, and the thousand year reign of Christ.

- Experiential, mystical Christianity is promoted to attract the postmodern generation. This includes changing the language of faith - i.e., not sin, but "mistakes" - not repentance, but "changing your mind" - not the Lord Jesus, but "leader and friend."

- As part of that effort to attract the world, cults, occult groups and Pagan religions are no longer referred to as such, but are called "sacred tribes," and Emergent leaders seek dialogue with them to see "what we share in common." Evangelism to them is considered an insult to the "sacred beliefs" of these "sacred tribes." (A common social engineering and dialectic consensus-building technique is commonly implemented under the phrase, "Let's see what we have in common, not what makes us different from one another, and let's find a common ground to dialogue." It is spiritually dangerous for the church to adapt this method of "dialoguing with the world." It always ends in us compromising Biblical truth in order to be acceptable to the world.)

- Scriptures, particularly the Gospels, are being reinterpreted according to the belief that we are here to "repair the world." For example, when the scriptures speak of those who "love His appearing" they say that if you feed a homeless person, you have brought the Kingdom to that person, and you have brought "His appearing" to them. Emergent thought continually downplays, disregards or reinterprets the Biblical concept of the literal second coming of Jesus in the clouds and appears to be implying that we - corporately - are the coming of Jesus. When they do, they are modeling their new theology after New Age leader Barbara Marx Hubbard, whose book *The Revelation* is a complete reinterpretation of the book of Revelation and presents the idea that the judgments of Revelation don't have to happen, if we all come together as one and embrace our divine destiny. I frankly find little or no difference between what Hubbard's "Christ spirit" laid forth and the "rethinking" of the Gospel presented by Emergent Church leaders such as Brian McLaren.

- The scriptures are being watered down and presented as "our shared stories." Scripture study is being replaced with power-point references on Sunday, and sensual, flesh-pleasing experiences, music and activities are being promoted as the key to experiencing God.

- A growing trend toward ecumenical unity for the cause of world peace, eradicating hunger, curing AIDS, etc. The Emergent Church is a social and political movement rather than a genuine spiritual move of God, as emphasis on evangelism, the Second Coming, taking a stand against sin and having a clear Biblical word is being replaced with a silence on those issues if not a denial of the importance of them, in order to do social good. But in spite of the fact that many Emergent writers want to paint the Emergent Church and its involvement in social causes as the new Jesus movement, as a product of and participant of the Jesus Movement of the 1970's, I can assure you, the Emergent Church is *nothing* like the Jesus Movement. The Jesus movement was born from the Spirit of God. The Emergent Church is born from the spirit of humanism.

- The church will begin to find that unity around the "Lausanne Covenant,"[1] which just recently presented the "Holistic Gospel of Christ" which emphasizes the "redemption of cultures" not people, and that the Gospel is about people having a "perfect bond with God" and "growing in every area of their lives." It says that we are given a "cultural mandate as well as an evangelistic mandate," and that the spread of the Gospel will lead to the "restoration of all nations." There is no emphasis on Jesus' coming, and rather than speak of man's sinful condition, it speaks of "disconnection of souls, clash of civilizations and confusion of truth." Renewal of "life, society, culture and all nations" is the goal of this covenant, NOT a call to repentance and preparation for judgment and Jesus' return. This covenant is a template that Emergent thought appears to be mirroring perfectly.

So pervasive has this covenant become that *Christianity Today* has said that "the unifying question is quickly becoming 'Do you subscribe to the Lausanne Covenant?'" This covenant is the New Age permeated Gospel of the Emergent Church that will unknowingly welcome the antichrist and a new world religious order in which TRUE evangelical Christians will be considered divisive, archaic and obstructive to the postmodern religious worldwide union.

Emergent Church leaders are numerous and prolific writers and speakers, and include people such as Rob Bell, Erwin McManus, Dan Kimball, Ken Blanchard, Dallas Willard, Brian McLaren and many others. There are many who are not directly identified as "emergent" leaders but nevertheless share in and carry their Globalist ideals such as Rick Warren, Robert Schuller, Tony Campolo and others.

It is this author's hope that rational and concerned Christians will study well this short guideline for identifying New Age and occult infections in the church and hold the line against it. While no one wants to promote a "witch hunt" just because someone might innocently use a few New Age terms in their writing or preaching, I have little fear that will happen. Rather, at this point, it appears that in churches all across the country, the foxes are not only guarding the henhouses, they are investing in poultry stock. Few are raising any warning, let alone a witch hunt. But every believer should divest themselves of the loaded terminology of the New Age and keep the message of Jesus pure from it. Using New Age terms in our preaching and teaching is not going to make us relevant. It will only make us vulnerable to the powerful occult and New Age "forces" behind their concepts. The church has its own vocabulary; it is the plain words of the Word of God, the scriptures. Let's use it, be known for it, and identified by it. Let us become once more People of the Book who are untainted by the seductive verbiage of the New Age movement and the emergent soup mess.

Chapter Three

First Lessons in Discernment

—‹‹‹›——

As she reached her hands towards him, Mack closed his eyes and leaned forward. Her touch was like ice, unexpected and exhilarating. A delicious shiver went through him and he reached up to hold her hands to his face. There was nothing there, so he slowly began to open his eyes.[1]

(Description of "Sarayu", an analogous character representing the Holy Spirit, from *The Shack* by William P. Young), Windblown Media, Copyright 2007, P. 208)

I walked into the front of the little church in a quiet neighborhood, reminding me of so many of the little Baptist, Pentecostal and Methodist churches I had spoken at over the years. I opened the white door and entered the foyer where tables with old felt-lined offering plates and visitors' cards were stacked.

The little church smelled old, but not musty. It felt homey and warm.

Inside the great room were seven or eight pews with hymnals in the back of them. I found a seat, and opened to the hymn they announced and sang along with everyone:

Only believe, only believe
All things are possible, only believe!
Trust Him and pray, believe it and say,
All things are possible, only believe

We sang two other very familiar hymns, rekindling fond memories of my early Christian experiences in little country churches growing up.

Then prayer requests were taken, and people gave testimonies. I heard someone speak in tongues, and miracles were spoken of, and healings as well.

"Now," announced the pastor as the lights were dimmed and a purple light on the wall near the altar was switched on, "we are going to channel the violet light for messages from God, and from our departed loved ones."

For the next hour, "messages" were "channeled" and spoken from "God" and the "dead."

Welcome to the spiritualist church.

Up until the last hour of that meeting, most Christians would not have known that anything was amiss.

They sang the right songs.

They had the right look.

They prayed the right prayers.

They operated in supernatural "gifts."

But NONE of it was from God.

Without true discernment, and at least some knowledge about the dangers of the occult, a weak Christian could easily be deceived by such a place. After all, these people were so *nice*. So *sincere*.

But when it comes to the shadow world of the occult and the New Age where deceptions and lies hide in even the most innocent places, nice and sincere are irrelevant. Truly, I have found many if not most New Agers, Wiccans and Occultists to be far nicer and sometimes *more* sincere than many Christians I have known. But that does not change the fact that they are bound in darkness and separated from Jesus Christ. Sincerity and niceness will not save them.

Sissy was a Christian counselor that a high school friend of mine was receiving counseling from. He was completely smitten by her love and wisdom. He wanted me and a friend from church to meet her. We did – and we were somewhat smitten too. She was extremely nice and very sincere. She had silver hair and a twinkly, mischievous smile.

Granted, there was a little knot in my gut saying something was wrong, but I couldn't pin it down. I hadn't yet learned that the "knot" was the Holy Spirit warning me.

I ignored the "knot." After a few meetings, Sissy invited us to a special prayer meeting with her mentor, a "very spiritual man."

When we arrived at Sissy's house, we met her mentor – tall, black hair, very nice but very imposing. He had a firm handshake, a steely smile and glistening eyes, almost shining.

He then proceeded to lead us in a "guided prayer." "Close your eyes and imagine a closed rose," he said soothingly. "Now count up, and one, two, imagine the rose opening its petals, three, four…" By this time the "knot" in my gut had become almost a scream to *stop*. In addition, I felt cold and dizzy and I began to shake. After counting to thirty he had us open our eyes, and he began to expound a message about the Christ Spirit, one that was *unquestionably* unbiblical and not from God.

"Stop this," I interrupted and his eyes flashed with Another's anger. "What's wrong?" he lovingly intoned in words that belied the cold, dark look in his eyes. "*THIS* is wrong!" I said. "All of it!" He and Sissy looked at each other sadly, and then looked at me condescendingly. "You're not ready for this step of growth," he said coolly. "Let's close the rose. Close your eyes, 29, 28, 27, imagine the rose closing…26, 25…" "Stop!" I yelled at my friends. "Don't close the rose! Stop it now!" The man's eyes were suddenly afire. "What-is-wrong?!" he asked again. "I'm freezing!" I said in a near panic. He smiled benevolently, knowingly. "That's the presence of the Holy Spirit!" he exclaimed. "No it is not!" I almost shouted. "I *know* the presence of the Holy Spirit – He's *warm*! This is SATAN'S presence!" Chaos ensued. The man stood up angrily to leave. Sissy looked hurt and wounded. We apologized for ruining the evening and left.

All the way home, my friend from church screamed and screamed from demonic attack, clawing at her skin as if to tear something off of her. It took us an hour of prayer to make it stop and restore her peace.

Sissy and her friend were so nice. So *sincere*. So…taken over.

In facing what is really behind the occult, secret religions and New Age, nice and sincere are irrelevant.

Only truth matters – and discernment.

That was one of my first lessons in discernment – to pay attention to the "knot" in my gut, the red flag of the Spirit that says something is wrong. Many times after that, I often felt something was wrong before I understood what it was. I would stop and pray when His warning gripped my gut. I wouldask for truth and clarity about the situation. When it came, and the matter became clear and was brought to the light of God's Word, the "false light" would be exposed and the demons behind the lies would scatter, leaving nice and sincere people angry, confused, and lost. Truth does that. It will set you free, but first it may make you furious. That is why our approach to people in that world must be full of compassion and love, because most of them truly are sincere, and the shattering of the lie they have followed can be truly devastating.

But today, the New Age and occult has come to our own gates, and few have discerned it or challenged it. There is a fog that has descended upon the church. It is a fog that makes truth cloudy and issues hazy and discernment unclear and difficult to obtain. It is a fog that comes from a shaky foundation of truth that is not grounded solidly in the Word of God. The Emergent Church reminds me very much of when Jesus spoke to Pilate about truth, about Himself. After being TOLD the truth, Pilate blankly asked, "What is truth?" as if Jesus had said nothing at all to him. His eyes were blinded to the truth. It is becoming the same with much of the church. A spiritual fog has descended on the church's mind, just like on Pilate's. The church today is ever learning, and never coming to the knowledge of the truth. The church is seeking after the new, the experiential and the exciting to the neglect of truth and faithfulness to the Word of God.

So much of the Contemplative/Emerging movement revolves around questioning what they believe, and questioning what they were *taught* to believe. That itself can be an indication that there may be little or no original encounter with the Lord Jesus who *is* the truth, or true surrender to Him which leads to radical change and eternal life.

In this coming New Age FutureChurch, there will be no simple reading of the Word of God and believing it. It will be about questioning truth, doctrine, and the scriptures. I asked a young friend who was surrounded by Bible school students who were drawn to the emergent ideas what the attraction was. He said, "They like to be able to question things." And we *should* be able to ask questions. Paul did say to "examine yourself, whether you be in the faith." (2 Corinthians 13:5) But he did *not* say, "Question the faith and the Bible and see if it's real." In fact, in the satanic world, Satan is known by another name: The Questioner. I'm concerned.

The FutureChurch will mock simple believers who just believe by "blind faith". But Jesus said, "Blessed are those, who having not seen, believe." It's OK to accept all of God's Word and not have to understand it all, or question it all. The simplicity of the Gospel is that you can come to Jesus and surrender your life in repentance, be born again of the Spirit, and become a new creation. Then you read the instruction manual and follow the instructions – the Word of God. In the Emergent Church, a whole generation of confused young people is allowed to skip everything about repentance, the blood of Christ, salvation through the cross and Jesus' sacrifice, and the need to abandon their all to Jesus and be born again. They just discuss what is relevant and right –or not - in their eyes, and they try to build a religious life around doing good works to "follow the way of Jesus." It's exacto-knife Christianity at best: skip what you don't like, change up what you do like to make it more palatable to post-modern sensibilities. The fog of confusion and spiritual uncertainty permeates and grips the Emergent movement.

I remember a creation science film I watched in Bible School which discussed the inner ear mechanism that keeps us balanced when we walk, but can also be easily knocked off balance through fluid in the ear, disorientation or various other means. The film told the story of a pilot that was lost in a fog. His instruments stopped working, so he flew by his instincts – by his feelings, so to speak. Based on the sensations and "feelings" he had (which he did not know had been totally disrupted and distorted by the fog), he believed with all his heart he was flying straight ahead in the right direction. But he was not. He was flying completely upside down and flew his plane straight into a mountain to his death.

Flight instruments are based on scientific truth and, barring a malfunction, do not fail. In the same way, the scriptures act as our instrument panel. If you "switch off" the solid guidance of scripture in exchange for experience and feelings, even a little, even a part, it can be spiritually fatal. God's Word is truth and it does not lie and it has never led anyone astray.

Rob Bell, Emergent Church leader and author of *Velvet Elvis* and *The Sex God* and creator of the *Nooma* DVD series, suggests that truth is like the springs on a trampoline, flexible. He says that people whose faith is dependent on "brickianity" – i.e., inflexible truth – do not really have a strong faith. He suggests if someone's faith can be shaken by, say, the possibility that the virgin birth may not be true, then they really don't have much of a real faith.

Bell's thoughts on "flexible truth" are an amazing and scary twist of logic which reminded me of a lesson I learned years ago.

I was working construction in California. It was a brutal winter, and we had put up several layers of a block wall in driving sleet and rain in 35 degree weather, carrying, measuring and laying over two hundred 75-pound cinder blocks.

On the third day, the boss came and measured. "Tear it all out and start over." "What's wrong with it?" we protested. "It's an 18th inch off at the foundation." "So?" I replied, every aching bone and muscle in my body crying out for vengeance. Then it was as if time stopped and God said, "Listen carefully to what he is about to say." His reply was a spiritual revelation about the nature of truth in our Christian walk:

"If you are off even a fraction of an inch at the foundation, eventually the whole wall is going to collapse."

So yes – if you treat truth like a spring rather than a brick, you have problems. You may be able to have fun on a trampoline but you cannot build a building on it. *The foundation of truth cannot be tampered with.* If you start pulling at the thread and being careless with the very sure measure of the Word of God, your whole faith will eventually either collapse or open the door to lies and deception.

There is a built-in fog of confusion and spiritual instability among those who question rather than just accept the truth of the Word of God. For those who would have spiritual stability and eternal fruit, the Word of God *is* enough. The kind of questioning (or, "rethinking") that Emerging Church leaders promote is being foisted on a generation already half-brainwashed by a New Age worldview that has been pushed on them, if not bottle-fed to them, since they first entered the educational system. It has literally been crammed down their throat in college and even in seminaries that are so antichrist in their view of the Judeo Christian faith, that kids under its influence who already have strong doubts about whatever Christian foundation they were raised with will simply add the new questions to the old and eventually just cobble together a religious experience made of patches of truth, threads of reality and a border of questions and come up with – exactly what the New Age wants them to - exactly what the New Age is – a religion in which *all* truth is right, except those who claim that Jesus' way is the only way to the Father.

It is not easy to write unpopular things about wildly popular movements like the Purpose-Driven Church, the Seeker-Friendly Movement, and the Emergent Church. To raise concerns about teachings and movements will by nature cause us to raise concerns about those who *forward* and *promote* these movements. Concerns about Purpose-Driven and Seeker-Friendly teachings and movements will by necessity bring concerns about Rick Warren, Bill Hybels and others in that movement. Concern about Emergent Thought by necessity will bring concerns about its proponents: Erwin McManus, Rob Bell, Dan Kimball, Brian McLaren, etc.

It would be easier to just say nothing. The necessity comes from the sad fact that so few even *question* the Biblical integrity of any of these leaders or movements that you cannot find one major Christian outlet – television, radio or Christian bookstore chain - that will give any voice to these concerns, or even *see* it as a concern. (But then, most of the major Christian media outlets are owned by secular corporations, so perhaps it is not a surprise that these things are not being addressed.)

It must be clearly understood that these concerns aren't questioning the sincerity of the people involved. Remember – sincerity and niceness are not relevant to truth. Truth is what it is. And Hitler was certainly sincere, was he not?

Nor is any of this meant to be a question about their spiritual lives. One can only judge the words next to the Word of God. Only God knows people's hearts. But this IS about truth, and in matters of truth, as I said, sincerity and niceness are irrelevant. A thing is either true or it is not. The messenger is not the primary issue. God's focus is on truth alone. Their focus is on their feelings, and truth is often abandoned in the pursuit of feelings and experiences that "feel right."

But, because the people that preach and promote these teachings are intimately involved with their message, they *do* matter. And they matter precisely because of the popularity, power and personality influence they have with a large and growing section of the evangelical church, and especially the youth and college age.

Some would say, "You shouldn't name names. The Bible says, 'Touch not mine anointed and do my prophets no harm.'" Were they prophets, perhaps I would pause. But they are not. We should remember that in the New Testament, when necessary, names *were* named. Paul said, "And their word will eat as doth a canker: of whom is Hymenaeus and Philetus." (2 Timothy 2:17) "Alexander the Coppersmith hath done me much harm." (2 Timothy 4:14) "I withstood Peter to the face, for he was to be blamed." (Galatians 2:11) There *is* a time to do so, painful as it is, because our love for the truth and our love for our youth should supersede any fear of offending someone, famous or not. If someone is teaching errors and lies and half-truths that are being touted as solid Christian teaching for our kids, and we know in fact it is poisoned, are we not obligated not only to identify the poison, but warn people away from those who serve that poisoned food?

Even the Bereans put Paul, the most well-known and well-written Apostle to the test, saying that they eagerly received the message but *searched the scriptures daily* to "see whether these things are so." (Acts 17:11)

Part of the reason that the church has come to this place is that the post-hippie generation that had come to Jesus and was once on fire for God eventually, because of weariness and discouragement, began seeking ways and methods to make big churches out of floundering little ones that people simply weren't interested in anymore. Part of their compromise was to accept and begin to use and promote these new programs and movements that, more than anything, have given the teaching of the Word of God such a tiny place in spiritual church life that kids who are now raised under these models of church don't even understand the *basics* of the faith, because most of them have not met the *author* of their faith through abandoned surrender to the Cross of Jesus, without which there is neither salvation, nor even a way to understand truth.

And that is my concern. We are promoting big leaders and big movements and wildly popular pop Christian books but no one is really looking at whether they are solidly grounded in scripture and truth. The fact that the vast majority of new youth pastors I have known are wild about all things Rob Bell makes me spiritually sick to my stomach, since even a cursory reading of his material or viewing of his DVD's with an ounce of discernment makes it plain that this is *not* the Gospel that Paul and the Apostles preached, and that millions have laid their lives down to defend. How do they not know that? Has the genetic component of discernment been programmed right out of this generation due to neglect and non-use, like an appendix that has simply shriveled to nothing?

It does not matter how nice people are. The criterion for truth is not niceness, nor popularity, but how what they say lines up with the scriptures. What saith the Lord? If there is a problem with the foundation, or the source of one's teachings (i.e., Rob Bell's spiritual role model, Marcus Borg, who does not believe the Bible is the perfect Word of God but a human product) then the person's popularity and charismatic personality do not matter.

If I were drowning, I would not care how mean my rescuer was. I'd prefer someone dragging me out of the water and calling me a fool idiot for diving in the deep end to someone who smiled benevolently from the shore waving and shouting, "Well, that's your experience, who can say it's wrong?"

Why is it important that we get beyond the outward appearances of the people behind the teachings? Because Paul said Satan can appear as an angel of light and his servants as ministers of righteousness. (2 Corinthians 11:15) I am afraid most Christians (if they even believe in Satan, and that's another chapter) expect Satan to appear in red underwear and a pitchfork and a tail. No, Paul said. He's going to look like...*us*. And, Paul said, "If I, or an angel from heaven, or any other person preaches any other gospel than what you have received from us, let him be accursed." (Galatians 1:8) Even me, Paul said. I am not more important than the truth. Truth comes first. Are we not obligated to examine the teachings these teachers are trying to mold our next generation of believers and leaders with?

Paul placed truth above personality and popularity. I have seen churches and teachings that looked 98% like they were from God. And those behind them were some of the nicest people I've ever met. But as one person said, if you eat something that has 99% good food and 1% poison, you can still end up 100% dead. That is the way it is with the FutureChurch theology that is riddled with half-truths and New Age lies. Some teacher, some movement or some spiritual activity may be 99% good – but if it contains 1% lie, you can still become 100% deceived. That's the nature of deception. It grows like a cancer. Satan is the father of lies, was a liar from the beginning and still lies, even if he puts on an evangelical suit or a clerical collar. Deception is his most potent weapon. It will be his final weapon.

Frankly, if my closest pastor friends begin teaching twisted truth, my love for the truth would *compel* me to act even if it cost me my precious friendships.

Our inability - or unwillingness - to do the same has allowed warped teachings and twisted truth to thrive among a generation who as been taught to "make nice" and overlook questionable and even anti-scriptural teachings in the name of unity.

It is a compromise we can no longer afford to make.

Chapter Four

A Failure to Discern

—⟋⟍—

"I need to talk to you about your book," a mother of one of the young people at the youth center I was involved with told me one night when I was busy playing one of the kids on a videogame. My book chronicled my involvement in the occult world before being delivered by Jesus.

We got into a back part of the building where it was quiet. "Fire away," I said, not knowing what to expect. "Talk to me about Edgar Cayce," she asked. Now, there was someone I could discuss. Along with Bishop James Pike, Edgar Cayce was a man whom I had previously followed, read all of his teachings and his writings had convinced me that being a Christian and a medium were not incompatible. Only after I became a Christian, learned the scriptures, and was delivered from the lies that had deceived me, did I come to know Cayce was a false prophet. Nice, yes. Sincere, yes, but nevertheless a false prophet. False prophets rarely know that is what they are.

"Edgar Cayce was an occultist," I told my friend's mom. "But he taught the Bible!" she exclaimed. I paused. "But, he was an occultist," I restated. "But he healed people!" she said, with a look of desperation in her eyes. I paused again. "But he was an *occultist*," I said very deliberately. "Oh dear God," she said as her face turned ashen white. "I'm in big trouble."

She proceeded to tell me about attending a ladies' Bible study at a good, solid church whose pastor I had known for years. The study was held by the wife of one of the oldest and most solid elders in that church.

After a number of months, the elder's wife invited my friend and a handpicked few other ladies to a more private, "deeper life" kind of group study. They went eagerly. But within a short while, she realized something wasn't right.

The teacher began to introduce Edgar Cayce's teachings to them. She taught them that the Bible contained the words of God, but wasn't perfect. Soon she was teaching reincarnation. In fact, she told them that she had been married to the High Priest Melchizedek over a million years ago on another planet.

When I spoke truth to my friend, the terrifying reality of how deceived she had been hit her with full force. She immediately made plans to cut all ties with this woman and her "Bible Study" group.

How did she end up in that place? One, her knowledge of the Bible's clear teachings about reincarnation and the occult practices that God forbids was nearly non-existent. It wasn't really her fault; it isn't taught in most churches, and hasn't been for quite some time.

But more importantly, she was ensnared because she trusted her teacher, who was well-respected, in her sixties, and she and her husband had a sterling reputation. And she was so sincere. And nice. Who was *she* to question someone with credentials and history, someone who had taught the Bible for decades? Maybe, she reasoned, it was just her problem, not her teacher's. Maybe, she thought, she just wasn't deep or mature enough to get these "greater truths."

This is how error and spiritual deception grows in the church unchecked.

I have a rule with the youth I teach. If I am wrong, if I misquote, or if I am teaching a half- truth or a lie, I make it clear that they are responsible to *call* me on it. It is their duty to do so, not just for them, but to protect others. I will not be like some who say, "Who are you to question me? The Bible says to 'touch not Mine Anointed'." Truth supersedes my position, my power and my pride.

I am glad my friend woke up and left her "teacher." But what disturbed me most was that her teacher was a woman who was well-known in church circles throughout the entire city. She was deeply involved in the intercessory prayer movement. And she had laid hands on and prayed for nearly every pastor in our city! And yet, she had not been discerned, nor discovered, nor confronted, nor stopped.

Where is our discernment? If we cannot discern and deal with such a blatant matter, how can we ever hope to deal with the little foxes, the little tampering with truth that are seeking even now to unravel the whole tapestry of truth within the church? And how then can we expose the bigger lies that even now are beginning to wrap their tendrils around the Body of Christ?

Chapter Five

The Future Youth: Defining "Christian" for the Next Generation

—⁓—

S ometimes I feel like I woke up to a spiritual nightmare. I do not recognize the church anymore.

I love the church. It's not always easy. Christians can be very unlovable at times. So can I. But we are His body, according to scripture. That is, those who belong to Him.

That's the part that's gotten cloudy and confused. The definition of what a Christian is has changed so much in my lifetime that "Christian" barely has any meaning anymore.

I live in a town where almost everyone goes to church on Christmas and Easter. If you ask them if they are Christians, they will say yes because they were born into a religious family that also goes to church twice a year.

But being born into a religious home doesn't make you a Christian any more than being born in a donut shop makes you a cop. Neither do two or three visits to church a year.

So what constitutes a Christian? A lot of people think it is a belief system. Some think it is someone who hates abortion and homosexuality, votes Republican and protests adult video stores. Others think it is someone who doesn't spit, swear, chew or go with those who do. Is that it? Is it about moral causes and moral living? No. Alcoholics Anonymous can get you to quit drinking but only God can change the heart. *It's not just about changed behavior.*

So, is being a Christian "following the way of Jesus," which is the new Emergent Church definition of Christianity?

Maybe I shouldn't, but I want to grill people who say that. What do you mean when you say you want to follow the way of Jesus? "You know, love people, feed the poor, that kind of thing," and that's usually about it. Just vague descriptions of nice deeds, proving what a great missionary once said, that most Christians are about a mile wide and half an inch deep. If you look at it, Jesus fed the people twice – at least that's what was recorded. We're not even sure they were poor; though it was likely they weren't rich. He loved prostitutes, tax collectors, thieves on a cross. But He had an anger that blazed at certain towns! "Woe unto thee, Chorazin! Woe unto thee, Bethsaida! For if the mighty works had been done in Tyre and Sidon, which have been done in you, they had a great while ago repented, sitting in sackcloth and ashes. But it will be more tolerable for Tyre and Sidon at the judgment than for you." (Luke 10:13-14) Seeker-Friendly churches would *never* have Jesus come to preach. He was far too offensive. Emergent Churches would not want him either; they would say he was unloving and judgmental, a "hater." There was far more to Jesus than doing good deeds and there is far more to being a believer or "follower of Jesus."

But yes, feed the poor! Care for the widow, the orphan, AIDS victims! (Just for the record, I was calling for the church to minister to AIDS victims *long* before Kay and Rick Warren and the Emergent leaders made AIDS a Gospel cause and priority, so do not think me unloving for writing these things.) Love is, yes, caring for AIDS children a world away – and we should and *must* – but though it is costly financially, it is not *difficult* love. Loving and caring for an AIDS victim in person – perhaps even one who may have contracted it from engaging in activities that we find morally wrong – not so easy. Do that, and *then* speak of "following the way of Jesus." The new Emergent Church definition of following Jesus sounds more like Gandhi speaking than a true believer. There are plenty of Buddhists and Hindus who "follow the way of Jesus" – taking what they like about what He said and disregarding the rest. Jesus was not Gandhi. Jesus was the Prince of Peace, but He said, "Think not that I am come to send peace on earth: I came not to send peace, but a sword. For I have come to set a man against his father, a daughter against her mother, and a daughter-in-law against her mother-in-law; and a man's enemies will be those of his own household." (Matthew 10:34-35) *He is not here to bring world peace.* The scriptures make it plain that when people said "peace and safety" then sudden destruction would come upon their heads. (1Thessalonians 5:3) The peace Jesus brings, He said, is not as the world gives. (John 14:27) The world grants temporary peace between nations, truces between countries. *His* peace is a peace that only comes through the forgiveness of sins through the cross. *Jesus did not come as a political reconciler.* He made it very clear that his kingdom was *not* of this world. (John 18:36)

So if you believe being a Christian is "following the way of Jesus," go all the way then. Follow His example in cleansing the Temple of God of its gross materialism, but *also* of its compromise and immorality! Follow Jesus and love the wicked but then have the guts to pronounce a word of rebuke and even judgment if He so demands!

When I hear Emergent Church leaders defining a Christian as "following the way of Jesus," it becomes pretty clear by their words and writings that either they haven't really *read* what Jesus said and did, or they simply took the parts of Jesus' life and words that were socially, intellectually and emotionally appealing and took an exacto-knife to all the rest and discarded it, leaving a perfect cut-out of "Chairman Jesus," the socialist-Ghandi prototype for the New Age Christian. Based on their definitions, being a Christian is mostly a socialist manifesto for the postmodern age, and not a transforming encounter with the Living God through Jesus Christ the Lamb slain for our sins.

I hear this talk and I think, What Jesus are you reading about anyway? Some of the things Jesus said scare me *far* more than anything I've read in the Old Testament! "Deny yourself. Pick up your cross and follow me...anyone who puts his hand to the plow and turns back is not worthy to be my disciple..."

Or how about this from Revelation: "I gave her space to repent... I will throw her on a bed of infirmity...I will kill her children with death..." (Revelation 2:22-23) Do you still want to follow *that* Jesus?

If we *really* want to follow the way of Jesus, we will be hated for the truth as He was, crucified for standing up to lies and telling the truth about a real hell that is the eternal destiny of those who do not believe. "He that believeth and is baptized shall be saved; but he that believeth not shall be damned." (Mark 16:16)

Do you believe that, do you believe all of it, or not? If not, you need to stop fooling yourself into believing you are really following the Way of Jesus. If you follow what you like and disregard or reinterpret what you do not, you are no different than Madame Blavatsky, Barbara Marx Hubbard, Marianne Williamson and every other New Age leader that has ever been. They too follow the parts that agree with their occultic understanding and world view. They disregard or reinterpret the rest. Do you really want to be in that company?

When you really start to take the words and example of Jesus seriously, prima facie, then you find that it is not easy, nor is it popular. I was taken aback by Emergent Writer Dan Kimball's book title, *They Like Jesus but Not the Church*.[1] Jesus never *asked* people to like Him. There were plenty who liked Jesus a lot, but they failed to follow Him. Follow Jesus in truth, and they will not like *you* either.

So I do not believe that "following the way of Jesus," at least as it has been defined by the Emergent Church, is being a Christian. So what is being a Christian, then?

It's not going to church. It's not being moral. It's not following a social ideal of a mystical Jesus who did good deeds. It is about whether you *know* Jesus. That is the real definition of being a Christian. It is about whom you *belong* to. Do you belong to Jesus? Are you, as Bob Dylan so pointedly wrote, the "Property of Jesus?" Isn't that what Paul defined being a believer as? "For you were bought with a price. Therefore glorify God in your body and spirit which are God's." (1 Corinthians 6:20) It is not what you believe as theology or philosophy, nor what you follow as a moral or social code, but *who owns you*? That is the crucial question. And I am afraid in the murky uncertain waters of Emergent Soup, those questions are not even posed. These are questions that cut to the heart of the matter. That is why I believe it is a matter of the *heart*. You should *know* if you know Him or not. You should *know* if you are His property or not, whether He owns you or not. If you are not sure, you can be. Being a believer is about total surrender to the Lord Jesus and receiving His blood sacrifice in payment for your sins and your ransom from eternal hell. It has nothing to do with whether you fail or do well, or have all the specifics right. It has to do with whether you have truly had a life-changing moment where you recognized Jesus was knocking on the door of your heart – and you let Him in – and turned over the keys to your *all* to Him. That is something you can know with absolute certainty. "He who comes to me I will in no wise cast out." (John 6:37)

We are entering into a time when Christianity is being completely redefined according to culture and personal preferences. The lines between the Way that Jesus truly gave us and the many other "ways to God" are becoming so vague as to leave an entire generation swimming in a sea of doubt and spiritual insecurity, doing a lot of nice things and hoping somehow it is enough.

It breaks my heart. This is an hour when we need to lift up the banner of truth that can give a kind of spiritual backbone and bravery to a generation that has suffered from two previous generations of spiritual recklessness, laziness, excess and "easy believe-ism" that has led them to know there is more – but turning to leaders who are as lost as they are and coming out with a confused mix of philosophy and theology that has neither certainty *or* backbone. We need to lift up the certain word of truth that is plainly outlined in God's Word.

A Christian is one who *belongs* to Jesus – who has given their entire life to Him – and who is in relationship with Jesus, a relationship so real and so complete and profound that everything else pales next to Him. It is a daily relationship through prayer and His Word that puts every detail of our lives in His hands, every decision in His will and every thought in His captivity. You can know Him this way. He wants you to. "This is eternal life... that they might know thee the only true God, and Jesus Christ, whom thou hast sent." (John 17:3) "These things have I written unto you that believe on the name of the Son of God; that ye may know that ye have eternal life, and that ye may believe on the name of the Son of God." (1John 5:13) You can be certain and put an end to the "conversation about God" that leads to confusion and "ever learning and never able to come to the knowledge of the truth." (2 Timothy 3:7)

You can know. Don't you want to know? And then you can help lead a lost generation out of the Emergent darkness and into the certainty of truth.

Chapter Six

The Neutralization of the Church

—m—

Jesus said the gates of hell would not prevail against the church. The real church is made up of those who gather together in His Name to do His Will and spread His Gospel. And truly, that church will not fail. But then, that must mean that much of what we see in Evangelical, post-modern, emerging religious circles is not "the church" but rather a form of religion that has the word trappings of the church but has not the power, nor the mandate, nor the authority that comes only from the Word of God and the power of the Holy Spirit. It is just a physical shell made up of lost people who for some reason have been drawn to a religious place and religious ideas but have not been drawn into total abandonment to Jesus and surrendered to His absolute Lordship. They are those Paul speaks of who have "a form of godliness but deny the power thereof." (2 Timothy 3:5) This is why Paul told us to "examine yourselves, whether you be in the faith" (2 Corinthians 13:5) because obviously, even then you could be in the *church* without being in the *faith*. He then gave the criteria: Jesus Christ is *in* you, unless you are reprobate. In other words, if Jesus does not live *in* you, you are not His. Your life must belong to Jesus, lock, stock, and barrel.

"Accepting" Jesus is a modern invention. As one evangelist used to point out, Jesus doesn't have a self-image problem where He needs our "acceptance." We need Him to accept *us*, and He will only do that when we come to the cross and surrender our old lives. I fear that much of the modern church is a group of nice people who are attracted to the nice ideas of Jesus and family and church but have never been to the altar, nor cried out for His mercy and forgiveness for their sins, nor surrendered their lives over to His Lordship. And that, as the last chapter explained, is what being a "Christian" is.

The modern church mix is made up of many people of the first order who are drawn to the ideas and trappings of church, but who have not given their lives to Jesus, and those of the second, those who *have* surrendered to Jesus at some point, but who have grown weary in well-doing and have laid down their mantles as watchmen and simply allowed all the new changes in "church" to come in without examining it and without contesting the wrong in it, and without taking a stand against the increasing infiltration of occult and New Age poison because they are…worn out. And the third group is a small group who know what is coming and who are being marginalized because they raise the warning cry.

In order for the One World order/One World religion to succeed and make the way for the antichrist to come to power, the first group has to be officially recognized as the "church," the second group of real believers needs to be neutralized, put to sleep or worn out to be too weak to fight, and the third must be marginalized, criticized, mocked and dismissed so they will no longer be part of the FutureChurch but will be considered outcasts, extremists and haters.

This is how it will be accomplished:

1. They will change the vocabulary of the church.

Much like a spiritual Orwellian nightmare, the "antiquated and alienating" language of the church will be replaced with a whole new dictionary of catch-phrases, cute and pithy rhyming bromides, tips and spiritual soundbites, as well as New Age-friendly and interchangeable words and phrases. Not acceptable will be the words sin, repentance, the coming of Jesus, tribulation, heaven, eternal life, judgment, the cross, the blood of Jesus, suffering, chastisement, the Lord Jesus. Instead, the new church dictionary is going to be made up of modern words and phrases designed to connect us to New World thinking and get us all "on the same page" (to use one newspeak phrase) and includes these weak and powerless substitutions for "that old time religion" talk: paradigm shift, emergent, enlightenment, transformation, Seeker-Friendly, dialoguing, sacred tribes, (instead of cults and witches and Pagans and Satanists) Jesus as Leader and Director (not Lord), Kingdom Now, Kingdom Come, As Above So Below, world changers, dream seekers, vision casting, changing direction or changing our way of thinking (instead of repenting), centering, contemplative prayer, dream catchers, reformation, etc.

Once all the words that have always defined and established the Gospel in not just words but power are eliminated, then this new vocabulary will become like an exclusive language that will make the "old talkers" look like outdated, unenlightened and non-progressive spiritual has-beens and relics from a less "transformed" time.

Since the New Age dictionary is the template for all the new Emergent "churchspeak," the new FutureChurch believers will indeed be on "the same page" – right out of Satan's playbook for absorbing and neutralizing the church. It will make that church as powerless as a toothless poodle.

2. They will gut the power of the Word of God.

This is being done through several means. First, they are glutting the Christian marketplace with new "translations," most of them based on a text pushed on the church by two British spiritualists (Westcott & Hort – check your translation and you may see their names in there. Google their names to find out who they were and what they believed. It is chilling) and has been the text that has been used as *the* text on which almost *all* new Bible versions are based. Then they throw in a glut of Bible "paraphrases" which are not translations but just a person's idea of what they think it means, such as *The Message*. As one of the most reliable (King James) translations becomes a relic that is unwelcome in the Emergent Church, Satan delights on seeing the look of confusion on people's faces as one verse goes up on Power Point and ten different people have ten different translations that aren't even close to what is on the screen – and they quietly conclude, "This is confusing. I'll just stop reading it for myself." This is why so few kids ever show up in church with a Bible. They just trust that whatever goes up on the screen is okay.

Being that hundreds of references to Jesus' Lordship, the Cross, sin and the Blood of Jesus are routinely removed from the new translations and paraphrases, soon the power and authority of God's Word will be taken out of the church and left with the few who dare to actually believe it *is* God's perfect Word. This new church and new "youth paradigm" will be one that uses scripture only as a "helpful guide." Kids will no longer be encouraged to "study to show yourself approved unto God," but instead will be fed experiences which will become more important to them than the Bible. The power and the importance of preaching and teaching will be downplayed and even mocked. (After all, they tell them, how many sermons do you really even remember?) This quest for experiences will become a gateway to massive deception, as one experience opens up to another. Those who challenge the experiences, if they do not line up with scripture, will be called Bible thumpers, extremists, Pharisees, and even those who are limiting the Holy Spirit.

As parents and church leaders stop putting a premium on the Word of God, kids will simply not take it seriously anymore. An encouragement to quiet time will become little more than a scripture bite with contemplative activities, breath prayers and other mystical devices that are merely Hindu practices in Christian disguise. The scriptures will become meaningless, or, at most, a nice guide to better living.

How far this is from the sacred Word of God that has cost millions of believers their lives just to possess even a portion of it over the centuries!

After enough new Bible versions have filled the church so that while we're all "on the same page," *no one* will on the same page, because the pages and words are so different. When enough "inclusive" language is put in the new Bibles to replace the old, there is going to come a New Age version that even Hindus, Buddhists, Wiccans and Pagans can accept. I believe it is already being worked on as I write. By the time it is brought out and hailed as the inclusive, definitive Bible for all ages, those who contend for the purity and authority of the Word of God will be so mocked and dismissed that they will be, to these FutureChurch believers, nothing more than a joke and an annoyance.

3. They must bring the church into Paganization through syncretism.

This is a program-in-progress even now, where, degree by degree, we lower the bar of truth in order to let unchurched people gain entrance – not to the Kingdom of God – but to this new church.

In this church, there will be no speaking of the occult or occult practices as bad, no talk of other religions as wrong, no speaking of Jesus as the only way. It will be the church that only accentuates the positive and eliminates the negative (positive and negative are also big newspeak words in this church) and its numbers will grow exponentially as people who are engaged in every sort of debauchery, occult practice and criminality will realize that this is a church that asks no questions, raises no standard and requires no repentance. Pagans will sit right next to pedophiles and petty thieves without any fear of being asked to change their lives. "Come as you are," the new banner, will never add, "Go and sin no more." There will be no discomfort, no challenge, and no conviction. This church will be big on works and become the perfect "model" for the One World order that will compel people to "heal the world" rather than prepare for Jesus' return. It will be a socialist club that will kiss the face of the Buddhist priest as they fall into eternal hell, join hands with the gay pastor and allow him to believe he is holy, and provide meeting places for those who engage in esoteric and occultic practices without one question being raised. As the church is being moved away from expecting a "pie in the sky by and by," and moved toward a socialistic works oriented religion that will take the place of social programs, it will be moving exactly into the place it was designed to by those who control the Luciferian agenda and do not want to eliminate the evangelical church, but neutralize, co-opt and absorb it. For this Luciferian order does not wish to destroy the world, but to make it a *perfect world* – disease free, poverty free, war-free – only with Lucifer as god and not Jesus as Lord of all. The move for the Emergent Church to be pushed toward "repairing the world" and be overwhelmingly involved in social and political causes is all part of the plan.

4. Lying Signs and Wonders Are Coming.

As the wall of truth is torn down and a "new way of understanding and interpreting truth" (or "rethinking") is put up with untempered mortar, I see a huge crack or gap in the back wall of the church. In the midst of this church will be souls hurting and hungry for the supernatural power of God. (As we should be hungry.) But there will be a multitude who are *not* exercised in the Word of God to discern truth from lie. They have not been taught, nor do they practice, how to "try the spirits, to see whether they be of God." They will seek an *experience* with God (as we should!) but the boundary of truth will not protect them because it has not been established *in* them through years of commitment to the engrafted and written Word.

This will provide a spiritual crack that is going to allow a trickle, then a stream, then a flood of false supernatural events to fill this new church. I am grieved and hesitant to say, that I believe much of this is going to come through the new "prophetic" movement.

I was spiritually raised up in a Pentecostal church and I believe in all the gifts and manifestations of the Holy Spirit. I believe we need them now more than any time in history. I am both an intercessor and a watchman, and have experienced the real power of God that has changed lives, healed the sick and set the captive free. I believe in *all* of God's Holy Spirit miracle power! And I long for it!

But I am also a former occultist, and I tell you before God, that Satan can imitate it *all*. I have heard tongues and prophecy and heard Gospel hymns and choruses in a spiritualist church. I have seen demonic healings and lying signs and wonders that would make the hair on the back of your neck stand up.

And I tell you, as much as I see the need for the prophetic and the miraculous and I believe much of it is from God, I am seeing that a great deal of it is *not*. Much of the flood of "words from God" is guessing, speculation, elaborate wordworking, and *untested*. The scriptures could not be plainer that we are to "believe not every spirit." I am concerned because a generation raised and conditioned and immersed in the occult through media and books *can not natu-*

rally discern an occult working from the Holy Spirit. And the door has opened to "satisfy" the "seekers of the supernatural" who do not, because they have not been trained to, "test the spirits." They are not being told to test the spirits, lest they be "doubting God" and "limiting the Spirit." This breach in truth will give way to lying signs and wonders, "sanctified" necromancy (that is already happening), meaningless miracles (what purpose does gold dust serve?) and direct "prophecy" from lying spirits. A church "open to anything" is going to fall prey to everything that is coming.

This particular phase is crucial to those who are "preparing the way" for "the One," as they call him, whose coming is with all lying signs and wonders. The FutureChurch will only see the power he shows and accept it without question as being from God.

I believe in the real supernatural power of God and miracles more now than I ever have. For that reason I raise this warning. *All that glitters is not God.* Test it *all*!

5. The final step: Eliminate the Apocalyptic.

None of the New Age agenda or One World/one religion can succeed unless the biggest obstacle is removed from the evangelical church as it stands: The preaching of the return of Jesus Christ in the clouds, the coming tribulation and the end of all things.

Tribulation, persecution, revelation, the second coming, the rapture, *all* that must be eliminated from the evangelical church's vocabulary and preaching and teaching if they are to succeed in absorbing it and creating the FutureChurch. And we're almost there *now*. Just this morning, I read these telling words from a "prophetic" conference: "We must stop this erroneous thinking about escaping with the rapture. Let's repent of this! Church mentality is *renting*. But God is into owning the whole thing!" (Meaning, the Earth.)

Here we see the crux of this new thinking: "Kingdom Now." "The Kingdom is *within* and *among* you!" "Thy Will be done on earth...now." Taking the true meaning out of Jesus' words – that we were to pray that God's will for redemption, salvation and healing be carried out here through our prayers and labors for the Kingdom - they have instead turned it into a mandate to ignore the reality of eternal matters and teach that we are to take over the planet and make it a paradise.

Many scriptures are being twisted and de-contextualized to condition the church not to expect Jesus' return (at least not from heaven and in the clouds) nor to prepare their lamps with oil, but to *take over*. It's called "dominion theology." It is going to send a whole multitude of naïve and non-discerning believers into a trap of thinking they are going to rule on earth but instead will face prison and a persecution of believers such as the world has never seen. Jesus warned us. You cannot read Matthew 24 and come up with the "heaven on earth" scenario that these new teachers are telling us to expect.

A thorough and honest reading of the New Testament makes it abundantly clear that Jesus will return in the clouds and that the church is to expect Him – to literally "love His appearing." (2 Timothy 4:8)The words of prophecy concerning the last days are abundant and numerous.

So why is it that this generation is completely unfamiliar with all of this? When was the last time you heard a message on Jesus' return or last days events or preparation?

I fear, for whatever good the "Left Behind" book series did, the damage may be greater, because now, well, it's all…fiction. Fiction stories.

In order for the coming antichrist rule to succeed, he must have a church that says, "Where is the promise of his coming? For since the fathers fell asleep, all things continue as they were from the beginning of the creation." (2 Peter 3:4) Are we not almost there now? Are not those who preach Jesus' soon return, who warn of coming tribulation and judgment, being categorized and dismissed as "doomsday preachers," people to be laughed at and mocked, or at least, cause people to roll their eyes at them in mild amusement and pity?

Watch for the Emergent Church to rapidly redefine and explain away and change the meaning of all the scriptures that deal with prophecy and the last days. And since most new church people don't read the Bible for themselves, the issue will rarely even come up.

Rather than pilgrims and strangers whose home is in heaven, who believe "to be with Christ, which is far better," who know the kingdom is invisible and who know we are not here to "heal the world" but to "call every man to repentance," this new church will become little more than the social relief agency for this coming world system of antichrist, and whose inclusion in that system will give them a false religious sense of purpose and destiny and doing good works, as they lose the true mandate: to preach the fiery gospel of Jesus because they know that "the end of all things is at hand."

It is difficult to believe, but the day will come when who Jesus was and is will be so redefined and changed, and what He said about His coming will be so twisted, that the "man of peace" – the antichrist - will come, and many of the new Emergent Church teachers will say, "We misinterpreted the scriptures. The Christ *has* come back, just not as we thought! He's come back as a human, and he's got the love, and the miracles, and the power to prove it!" And thus the deception – and the way that has been prepared for the end of things - will be complete, and the final countdown will begin.

I cannot bring myself to end this on a positive note, lest I detract from the gravity of what I have written and been shown. I will only say, to those who have ears to hear, hold your ground; be strong; behave like men and women of the living God; put on all your armor, watch, and earnestly contend for the faith that was delivered to you; keep your bags packed and hold everything lightly in your hands; preach the uncompromised word that makes people sweat, get angry, and walk away or repent and weep and get saved; do not compromise; prepare for hard times; and look up and rejoice, because your redemption is drawing nigh!

Man the outposts! Hold the line. Be the warrior. Do not back down. Stand firm in the truth, and the gates of hell will not prevail against those who stand and fight to the last!

Chapter Seven

Removing the Linchpin

—·vvv·—

Satan fears the Word of God. I've lived long enough to see the power of the Word of God change lives, heal the sick, deliver from demons, mend broken hearts, and set people on fire with purpose and power.

I recently agreed to do a phone interview for a magazine, innocently believing I was going to be asked about my work. Instead, it was a setup, and I was viciously attacked. At one point, the interviewer said, "You have no formal training. You've got some honorary doctorate from some podunk double-wide Bible College from the south! What right do you have to post what you do on the internet?" "Because it's the truth," I answered. "That's *your* truth!" they replied. I nearly laughed. I'd hit the crux of the matter. "Listen bubba," I replied, "There's no 'my truth' and 'your truth.' A thing is either true or it's not."

To rephrase a C.S. Lewis thought, if I said I was a poached egg, you would call a therapist. "But that's MY truth!" No, that's my *delusion*. Clearly I am not a poached egg, no matter how much I may believe I am.

Somehow, absolute truth has been completely lost in the modern lie of "relativism" – the idea that truth is subject to circumstances, social settings and personal feelings. One professor told a student, "There are no absolutes," to which the wise student replied, "Are you absolutely sure?"

The degree to which relativism has infested the educational system and filled young minds with lies is deeply disturbing. I can't even have a rational conversation with most "educated" people. They get emotional and angry when presented with reason and facts that contradict their oft-repeated and little reasoned ten second sound bite opinions, finally ending the conversation with, "Well, that's YOUR truth!" Which is the modern academic version of "Nanny, nanny, boo boo!"

Can you imagine, if, for example, driving laws were based on relativism?

-   The lights are red, yellow, and green. If your truth says red means go, then go.
-   The speed limit is only a suggested one. If it "feels right" to go 90 MPH in a school zone, follow your heart.

In other words, lawlessness and anarchy would rule the road, and it would be a slaughter when "your truth" opposed "mine" and we met in a fatal crash of relativistic speed limit interpretations.

Can you imagine if scientists worked by that standard? We'd never have gotten to the moon. "It's about a million miles...we think...but we only use the rule as a 'general guideline.' The moon looks closer by eye, so we trust that more than some 'absolute ruler.'"

Obviously we don't conduct science *or* road laws by relativism.

But we *are* told by the world to conduct our lives that way. Paul calls it "the spirit of lawlessness." It is the ageless satanic lie that says that you can become your own god.

Now that most of the world is under the influence of this lie, Satan has now set his sites on the church. The church has always been most powerful when it has proclaimed the pure Word of God. Satan knows it is his biggest threat.

For hundreds of years, he's been successful at weakening the church through petty doctrinal differences like methods of baptism, tongues, and end-time disputes.

Now, he's about to go for the jugular. He is seeking to completely destroy the standard of truth – the Word of God – in the house of God.

The Bible is the standard – the linchpin, so to speak – the foundation of truth by which we live. All else – relationships, righteousness, directions and destiny – hinge on it and our ability to stay true to it. God Himself set that linchpin – "Forever, O Lord, Your Word is settled in heaven." (Psalm 119:89) "Heaven and earth will pass away, but My words will never pass away." (Matthew 24:35) And woe to those who tamper with it!

But tampering they are, to their own destruction.

A young person I know attended a Christian Bible school where he was subjected to a book that contained a chapter that argued that the Bible really did NOT condemn homosexuality. Talk about confusing! You go to a Bible School to learn about the Bible, and they undermine the very thing they claim to stand for!

We used to joke about seminaries, calling them "cemeteries" and now I don't think we were too far off the mark. I will be accused of being anti-intellectual, which is fine. I've got to tell you, I've rarely seen someone argued into the Kingdom of God. Even the great C.S. Lewis came to Jesus by a burst of spontaneous revelation riding his bike, not by argument. People come into the Kingdom, not by good ideas, but because God opens their hearts to truth. And yes, there is a place for reasoned argument. But it always strikes me that although Festus said, "Paul, you almost persuade me to become a Christian," we don't know that he ever did.

My concern isn't just that we're too intellectual. In fact, there are too many believers that "only believe" but haven't a clue as to why. I always encourage kids to learn all they can, get all the facts and think sharp so they can "be ready to give an answer to every man for the hope that is within you." (1 Peter 3:15) Nevertheless, the rise of Christian intellectual elitism that is pervading many seminaries, Christian media and churches is a concern. I realize I am not a scholar. I can't argue didactic points (or even tell you what didactic means) or give grand outlines. I'm just a truth-teller. And I expect the world to react negatively to what I say and write. But 90% of the assault I get comes from Christians who think I'm too subjective, too "experiential." Much of the remaining criticism is that I am too "fundamental." I get it from both ends. But in fact, I stand in the middle and believe that experiencing God is totally compatible with

71

100% faith in the Scriptures: experience *and* scriptural knowledge. In fact, it is only when these things become one dynamic that the Kingdom is truly manifested in power.

But given the option of being too "fundamental" or too "experiential," based on the dangerous place I see a lot of Christians today, I'll take "fundamental."

For many, that translates as "Pharisee." But the Pharisees' problem wasn't that they believed the Scriptures; it's that (a) they added a thousand laws and inferences not there, and (b) they did not grasp the truth of the scriptures that *were* there. "You search the scriptures, thinking you will find eternal life; but these are they that speak of Me." (John 5:39)

In other words, they took the Word and tried to make it say what they wanted it to say. You can't do that.

I recently had a conversation concerning the scripture, "Do not be unequally yoked with unbelievers." (2 Corinthians 6:14) Someone had told a young person I know that it was referring to business deals, not marriage. (The logic of that, of course, is absurd – implying that God cares a lot about keeping our business dealings separate from unbelievers, but in the most spiritual human relationship of all – marriage – it doesn't matter!) I listened as this young person explained that this man had been living with an unbeliever, and she later got saved. (Maybe she did. I hope so and I'm happy for them if that is true.) The young man I spoke to asked if I thought that this man was in trouble with God; after all, he was doing well, and was financially blessed, his wife got saved – didn't that indicate God's blessing?

First, I explained, his finances were irrelevant. Second, I said, he's in more trouble than he knows. *He believes a lie*. Rather than take God's Word at face value concerning not being unequally yoked, he said, "It doesn't fit how I'm living. I've got to see it in a way that I can make it fit my lifestyle." Peter spoke of those who "twist the scriptures, to their own destruction." (2 Peter 3:16)

Worse – he was teaching kids the same thing! I would rather be living in abject sinful failure and proclaim, "I may be in sin, but the Word of God is still true" than to twist or distort the scriptures to cover up my violation of it. It's about integrity to truth.

Anytime we run into scriptures that speak in opposition to cultural sins or our personal ones – we choose to either receive the truth regardless, or we end up twisting what is there to make it support sin.

Never – *never* – bend the Word of God to accommodate or justify your sins or lifestyle. Bend – and break – your own hardened sinful heart and conform to God's truth. Fall on the rock and be broken, Jesus said, or it will fall on you and crush you to powder. (Matthew 21:44) "Is not my Word like a rock...like a hammer?" (Jeremiah 23:29)

If my experience contradicts the scriptures – my experience is wrong. Period. If my way of life contradicts it – my way of life must change. It's that simple.

I recently read an article by a mother about keeping kids away from the occult. She agreed with all the scriptures against it. Then she explained how she read Harry Potter with their kids, explaining the good, pointing out the bad. (Either make the tree good and its fruit good, Jesus said, or make the tree corrupt and its fruit corrupt – Matthew 12:33) She did the usual justification of the difference between real magic and fantasy magic.

Then, in a stunning piece of advice, she tells parents to steer children away from things that were about talking to the dead, divination or spell-casting! She apparently was completely blind to the fact that Harry Potter was *filled* with spell-casting, teachers who were divinators and the dead speaking through the living!

This is a perfect example of loosening the linchpin of truth even a little. She loosened it just a hair – "Well, the scriptures are probably only condemning real magic, not fantasy magic..." The next thing you know, in one breath she can tell you to avoid occult practices, and in the next, promotes a story *full* of them – without a *clue* to the contradiction! Once you loosen the linchpin just a little, it's just the beginning.

Someone told me, "I don't accept a certain part of the Bible." I said, "Well, then throw the whole thing in the trash and get it over with. Because if you can't trust that part, why trust any of it? How do you know any of it is trustworthy if you just throw out what you don't like or don't believe?"

No. Accept it *all* or accept *none*.

That doesn't mean it's all easy to understand. Far from it. Many times I feel like I did when I was a child, crying, yelling, staring at math problems and saying, "I don't get it!!!" How foolish to abandon math, thinking that because it does not always make sense to *me* therefore it must not be true. It's my understanding that is lacking, not the material.

I play a frustrating computer game where you have to combine similar objects to get points. As the clock runs down, I can rarely find the combinations to keep the game running. But it's *there*. On occasion, I just take a deep breath, relax, and tell myself, "You can find it. It's right there somewhere." And there it is. The game didn't lie; I just couldn't see what was there.

I've always approached the Word of God that way. If I'm confused or don't get something, I say, "The answer is here. Show me, Father." And He does. Sometimes the answer was right in front of me, but I was not able to see it without the Holy Spirit's help.

Math does not lie. It's fundamental truth. The Word of God does not lie; it is fundamental truth. Change one math fundamental, you produce chaos. Change one little iota of scripture, then spiritual chaos will follow.

In a time when many churches and even denominations are trying to remove the linchpin of the Scriptures to justify adultery, homosexuality, occultism, you name it, in a time when "new translations" are cool and the "old" are being buried by them, it is imperative that men and women of God who are charged to protect that linchpin of truth nail it in solid, guard it and *teach* it to this generation, who will be the guardians of the Word of God for the generation to come.

As an old preacher once said, "God said it. I believe it. That settles it." It's just like that. Anything less is tampering with the Word of God, to our own destruction.

Chapter Eight

East Meets West: Contemplative Prayer, Christian Yoga and Spiritual Deformation

—∿—

...the teachings of the east and west must be fused and blended before the true and universal religion – for which the world awaits – could appear on earth.[1]

Alice Bailey, founder of Lucifer's Trust

In 1977 I began to meditate, going to the hill behind my home in Washington DC each morning. I learned to say the Lord's Prayer in deep concentration. I started to regularly hear an inner voice. I recorded its message in my journal...[2]

Barbara Marx Hubbard, author of *The Revelation* and major New Age teacher, *The Revelation*, P. 55)

Meditate on the resurrected Christ....Empty your mind of all thoughts you do not think with me.[3]

Barbara Marx Hubbard, *The Revelation*

Sit in a quiet room in loose clothing and focus on your breathing.[4]

Trance-channeled "spirit," answering question posed by Esther Hicks about what the best way was to accelerate their growth in New Age practices and teachings. Esther Hicks later trance-channeled the "Abraham Group," which became the basis for Rhonda Byrne's *The Secret*.

In Yoga, one of the central tenets of Yoga, is your breath needs to remain the same, regardless of the pose... the Yoga masters say, 'This is how it is when you follow Jesus and surrender to God...' That's integrating the divine into the daily.[5]
Rob Bell, author of *Velvet Elvis*

Before I became a Christian, I was steeped in every kind of occult practice you can imagine. I read cards, levitated things, studied astrology, conducted séances and did astral projection – and that is just a partial list of my spiritual pursuits.

In the months leading up to my salvation, I dove headlong into Buddhist and Hindu scriptures and philosophy in a desperate attempt to find answers – to find God. I discovered a writer – Paramahansa Yogananda, founder of the Self-Realization Fellowship in California. I devoured his every word. I began meditating, doing breathing exercises, anything I could to put me in touch with the "divine within" that Yogananda – and Hinduism – taught that we all possessed.

I did not find the "divine within." Meditation led me into altered states of consciousness that only added to my confusion, where the line between the real and the unreal blurred. Instead of being filled with light and peace, I was falling further into absolute emptiness and darkness.

I am thankful it didn't work. If I had experienced the false light like most do while practicing meditation, I might have stayed on the path of Luciferian "light" for years and perhaps never come to Jesus. I'm so glad, after seven years of chasing the mystical tail and the labyrinth of death, He took me out of it all.

I was very spiritually messed up when I came to Jesus. When I first went out with an evangelism team, I handed someone a paper and said, "You need Jesus." One man said, "I'm a Buddhist." "That's cool," I told him cheerily. "All paths lead to God!" I would have fit in quite well in the Emergent Church whose leaders believe it is arrogant to claim Christianity is the only way to salvation. "You need Jesus!" I told another person. "Why?" he replied. "Will I go to hell if I don't believe in Jesus?" "No," I answered. "There is no hell. Heaven and hell are here on earth." I would have made a perfect "Kingdom Now" believer.

Thankfully, someone reported my "witnessing" to the man who led our house church. When we got back from our street outreach, he got out his Bible and made me read several Bible passages out loud that completely unraveled the foundation of my New Age beliefs in reincarnation, all paths leading to God, heaven on earth, and a host of other occult philosophies I had not yet been delivered of. I was angry and devastated.

But the door of truth had been opened. I went home determined to find scriptures that would support my Hindu/Buddhist/New Age worldview. What I discovered was exactly the opposite. It shook me to my very core, because after seven years in the occult, I had to face the fact that either the Bible was true, or my occult/New Age worldview was true, but not both. The occult and New Age teachings were completely diametrically opposed to the truth of the Bible, and I could not mix them even a little if I was to be a true follower of Jesus Christ. He did not leave the option for believing in any other way to God. He said plainly, "I am the way, the truth, and the life: no man cometh unto the Father, but by me." (John 14:6) The Bible did not leave any open door for reincarnation, or heaven on earth, or the "divine within" that I had been taught was already in me. After deciding I would believe the Bible no matter what it did to my previous convictions, I ended all my meditation sessions, got rid of my books, and took down my beloved Yogananda poster that read, "From Unreality to Reality; From Darkness to Light; From Death to Immortality; Om, Shanti, Shanti, Shanti." (Peace, Peace, Peace. None of it had brought me either true light, nor immortality, and certainly not real peace. Only Jesus gave me real light, peace and eternal life.)

For years I have watched as Eastern Mysticism has crept into our school systems, the media and our culture. I watched as a

Hindu entrepreneur, Maharishi Mahesh Yogi, took Hinduism and meditation, hooked the Beatles and dozens of Hollywood celebrities on it, and then somehow made it "scientific." It became "TM" - Transcendental Meditation. By way of the "boil the frog in the pot" method – a degree at a time so it does not notice – TM and Yoga were slowly injected into the schools via the ever-antichristian National Education Association and willing teachers who were now following the way of the East.

At first, parents objected to this exotic form of religious practice being foisted on their kids. And well they should have. But a religious practice – Yoga – renamed and "scientifically" packaged – slowly became acceptable, then normal, and now, commonplace and popular. Science has "proven" Yoga lessens stress and helps keep the body limber. Actually, just slowing down and taking deep breaths helps stress – a fact people knew long before Yoga became a cultural phenomenon. "Calm down! Just take a deep breath!" Right? And stretching, with or without Yoga, will help keep you in good shape.

Yoga, however, includes two other little features, one or both of which are introduced to new practitioners.

First, the poses, or "asanas." A number of them are prayers to Hindu gods, including the "sun pose" which is a greeting to the sun god. It's a little detail that Western style Yoga gurus and entrepreneurs fail to point out to new practitioners. And what are the poses meant to achieve? Swami Sivenanda Radha, a well-known Yoga teacher, has said in the book on Hatha Yoga, "Asanas are a devotional practice...each asana creates a certain state of mind...to bring the seeker into closer contact with the Higher Self."[6]

And what is that "higher self?" Hinduism teaches that it is the "divine within." Yoga practices are meant to create an altered state of consciousness by which you can achieve "God realization" – the understanding that God is all, and in all, and we are divine – we are God.

Then, there is the "mantra" – a little word you are given to repeat over and over again while breathing and stretching. "Aum" or "Om" is kind of a catchall for all of the Hindu gods, and by chanting it over and over, it invokes those gods and brings them close to your consciousness. Sometimes practitioners are given a mantra chosen from among the thousands of gods. Sometimes you are told to pick your own word. But it is the *repetition* that matters and the key to the experience. It is done to place you in an altered state of consciousness so you can experience the "divine within." And the breathing, in combination with the "mantra" and the poses, are done to awaken the "Kundalini" spirit (a Hindu female deity) – a serpent spirit they believe lies dormant at the base of the spine. Yoga's purpose is to awaken this serpent, which, while you have opened the door through attaining an altered state of consciousness via Yoga, will travel up through the seven "chakras" or "energy centers" of your body and explode into "light" and "self-realization" or "God-realization" through your seventh chakra, located in the "third eye" in the middle of your forehead.

And you thought it was just exercise.

My prayer is that, having read the above, a flash of brilliant light of the *God* kind called "truth" will jar you into reality and help you understand what dangerous doors can be opened through Yoga and TM.

If you have practiced these things, I would challenge you to sit down with a qualified Christian who can pray for you, for God to remove the effects of these practices. You may find there was more there than you realized.

But what does this have to do with Christians? I have always understood how dangerous all this was – both as a former practitioner and as someone who has worked in counseling and deliverance for years – but I never dreamed that in a short period of time, the church would become riddled with eastern Hindu and Buddhist philosophy and that "Christian Yoga" would not only become acceptable, but it would become a huge marketing item through the formerly Christian book publisher Zondervan.

When I first learned "Christian Yoga" was going to be pushed on the church, my reaction was, "You have got to be joking." But after a short time, I realized that nearly an entire generation had been raised without having a clue that there was anything spiritually wrong with Yoga or its attached philosophies. (A perfect example is how we have accepted the phrase, "What goes around, comes around" as a common expression that means, "You'll get yours," without understanding that it is a Hindu concept called "Karma" and is referring to reincarnation.) The church certainly wasn't warning people – we were too busy building big churches and engaging the political arena. This was a generation that would digest the idea of "Christian Yoga" without question because Yoga had never been questioned.

Yoga is a dangerous practice. It is a Pagan form of meditation whose express purpose is to open up one's "chakras" or energy centers to put one in touch with the "divine within." Every Hindu pose is a prayer to a Hindu god.

There is a lot of emphasis in Spiritual Formation, Contemplative Prayer, and Emergent Church circles about returning to the teachings of the "early church fathers." But the teachings and practices of the early church fathers are a mixed bag; some were insightful and astonishingly holy, but most were riddled with eastern mysticism, Gnosticism, and other philosophies which were highly occultic. The "church fathers" writings are very much an "eat the chicken, throw out the bones" proposition. (It's very similar to the majority of Christian writings today!)

But I am very concerned that we have made the "early church fathers" our template for the New Spirituality. The only template we can absolutely rely on for the "way to do church" is the New Testament, but particularly the Book of Acts. Because after the destruction of Jerusalem, you can trace the slow but deliberate elimination of the true church that was experienced in Acts and the transformation into a mix of Pagan culture and religious rituals. In the early church, they still were very much Jewish in their understandings, practices and temple attendance. The church met in homes. The leaders of the early church were apostles who led and lay down the foundational understanding of how church should work.

With the destruction of Jerusalem in 70 AD and the mass slaughter of Jews and early believers, temple attendance was gone, and the real church was scattered and underground – but very much alive.

Then came Constantine. His "conversion" is a matter of much debate. He saw a "cross of light" above the sun and heard the words, "In this, be victorious!" and subsequently, according to legend, Christ came to him in a dream and explained how if he used this sign of the cross, he would conquer his enemies.

First of all, the Acts church did not use the cross at all. They used the fish. Secondly, there is no real evidence that Constantine did any more than use a cross symbol to rally troops and become a conqueror. And even if it was a dream, are you really ready to believe that Jesus told him to take the cross and conquer, the same Jesus that said, "Put away your sword" to Peter?

Nevertheless, Constantine subsequently made "Christianity" legal - then mandatory. None of that was good for the true body of Christ that consisted of people, many Jewish, many Gentile, who belonged to Jesus and were spreading the Gospel even in persecution. In fact, the book of Acts made it plain that when the church was persecuted, they grew. When Constantine made Christianity the official religion, it began the slow decline of all that the Apostles died to defend. Soon the "church" was allowing all manner of Paganism into its midst, including choosing the Pagan holiday of Mithras for Jesus' birthday – thereby effectively de-semitizing it and taking the Jewish heart out of His birth, which some scholars say was more likely to have been in the fall, perhaps during the feast of tabernacles. Before long, the church was a mixed entity that contained those who were defending the faith, and those who were turning it into an open door of non-Biblical practices and concepts. The church then went on to carry out the bloody crusades. The history of the church after Acts was not a pretty picture. It was a war between those who sought to protect the purity of the faith once delivered to them and those who turned the church into a political, social, and financial organization that controlled the masses, kept them from reading the Bible and persecuted and murdered all dissenters.

This is the spiritual entity from which the Contemplative movement and Spiritual Formation is culling its spiritual heroes on how to find God. They follow writers like Thomas Merton, a Buddhist supporting priest. (Merton said, "I see no contradiction between Buddhism and Christianity...I intend to become as good a Buddhist as I can."[7]

They are drawn to Henri Nouwen, who admitted at the end of his life that he did not believe Jesus was the only way to the Father. He said:

Today I personally believe that while Jesus came to open the door to God's house, all human beings can walk through that door, whether they know about Jesus or not. Today I see it as my call to help every person claim his or her own way to God.[8]

These new leaders of the Contemplative Movement in the church were steeped in the writings of the "early fathers."

You need to know the history before you just accept the popular idea being pushed to "return to the early fathers" and realize that much of their teaching had very little to do with the way the early believers in the book of Acts taught, believed and lived. Much of what they wrote was exotic and extra biblical, and in many cases, tinged with mystic occultism and strange supernatural manifestations that the Bible does not teach, but the occult world is full of.

Neither Jesus nor the Apostles taught contemplative prayer, or "spiritual formation" principles, or "breath prayers" or techniques, or transcendental meditation. The prayer of the early church Christians was powerful, dynamic, and focused. Aside from Peter's "trance" experience while in prayer, there is absolutely no precedent for any of these exotic teachings on proper breathing, meditation, Christian Yoga or the new style of "contemplative prayer." We are told to meditate on God's word. Jesus said *not* to use vain repetition like the heathen did; saying a word over and over in "prayer" is vain repetition, and it is *also* "mantra" praying that is designed to get you, in combination with "breathing," into an altered state of consciousness. That is a complete contradiction to Peter's admonition to "be sober, be vigilant." Satan wants to lead people into some quasi-mystical state of meditation where they will become susceptible to all manner of delusions and spiritual lies. Read again the quote from the beginning of this chapter from Esther Hicks, trance-channeling medium who is responsible for the message of *The Secret*, one of the most highly occultic messages to receive widespread recognition in this decade. The "spirit" (demon) who answered her question about how to accelerate her growth in New Age spirituality told her to sit in a room in loose clothing and *focus on her breathing*. That led shortly to her *own* possession by "ascended masters" (demons) who use her as a vehicle for their New Age message. The new teachings on "breath prayers" and "Christian Yoga" are indistinguishable from what is taught in Hindu Yoga and through "ascended masters." Doesn't that alarm you? It really, really should.

I have had dreams from God. I have seen visions from God. *None* of those were achieved through any technique, or my imagination, or proper breathing, or sitting in a correct posture, or surrounding myself with stuff. They were the result of prayer, speaking heart to heart with God as a friend and my Lord and pouring out my heart in a real and completely open manner. I didn't have to do anything at all. Most all significant revelations I have ever gotten from God were while I was reading and meditating on His Word. If you do things God's way, He will draw near, He will speak to you.

But when you use occult and eastern religious techniques as a way to make you "aware" of God, you are on dangerous ground. Contemplative Prayer teaches you these techniques in order for you to look "inward" to discover "God in you." Buddhists and Hindus teach the same thing. When you use these techniques - which the scriptures do *not* teach - to attain a spiritual goal, the goal you attain will be the goal that those who *teach* those techniques want you to: "divine realization" – that God is everywhere, and in everyone and everything – which the Bible does *not* teach. But Pagans and eastern mystics do. It's known as panentheism. The Bible does not teach that we are divine. It only teaches that believers in Jesus can know "Christ in you, the hope of Glory." That doesn't mean we are God, but that Jesus came to live in us by the Holy Spirit – not some divine energy, not the "cosmic Christ spirit," but the literal *person* of Jesus Christ the Savior and Lord who lived, died and rose from the dead 2,000 years ago.

People who practice Contemplative Prayer and "breathing" which are based on eastern occult teachings – no matter how "Christianized" someone has tried to make it – will receive the result of opening themselves to the spirit of deception and false religions and a false Christ spirit. You cannot do something that is fundamentally wrong because it is based on Pagan and occult practices, Christianize it and get a "Christian" result. You will get the result that comes from disobeying the scriptures that tell us to *not* adopt the religious and occult practices of the lands we are in but to come out from among them and be separate and "touch not the unclean thing." (2 Corinthians 6:17) Guided visualization, breathing techniques, and Yoga meditation are unclean occult practices that are taught in New Age classes and centers around the world. You cannot do an ungodly thing that is the foundation of the New Age and occult world and turn it into a good thing. Remember, Jesus said make the tree good and the fruit good, or the tree evil and the fruit evil. Planting the seeds of Contemplative Prayer as it is currently being taught and other eastern religious practices disguised as Christian into Christian soil will produce a spiritually poisonous tree.

If you have practiced any of these things in ignorance, you need to ask Jesus to forgive you and cleanse you. You may also need a pastor or Christian counselor or minister to lay hands on you and pray for God to deliver you from the demonic entities that may have attached themselves to you or surrounded you as a result. That is likely, because in the demonic world, if you call them, they will come – and eastern meditation is one of the easiest ways to get their attention. It takes you out of the presence of the Holy One and opens a clear door for them to influence your mind which has been put in a stage of altered consciousness because your spiritual guard has been taken down. You need prayer.

One of the most effective ways that the New Age has been able to weaken the true power of God in the church is to have Christians buy into Christian Yoga, Contemplative Prayer and "Spiritual Formation" without discernment, without knowing what the Bible says about these things, or about how deeply entrenched in occult and New Age practices all of it is. At the least, it is creating a spiritually unhealthy and crippling obsession with one's own spirituality, rather than causing believers to go outward to share the Gospel with others. At the worst, it is creating a mass "altered state" among believers who practice these things, and eventually will put them "on the same page" with all the very spiritual-sounding and even Christian-sounding New Age teachings that are beginning to flood our media – even the Christian media – and rendering the church powerless to fight against the deception at our gates, even now.

Chapter Nine

Velvet Elvis or False Jesus?

—ɷ—

"You have to see this, it's awesome!" I was handed a DVD by a friend. It was called *Bullhorn*, part of a series of DVD messages titled *Nooma* by someone I had never heard of, Rob Bell. Because I am always looking for good material for kids at youth group, I got home and eagerly plugged it in. From the moment I began to watch it, I felt nauseous and didn't know why.

The DVD began with Rob Bell, casually dressed and hip looking, sitting on a park bench, interspersed with scenes of an older street preacher, wearing thick glasses, scared of people, printing literature and going on the streets with a bullhorn to preach. The portrayal of this man as an unattractive, outdated offensive relic could not have been clearer, nor could Mr. Bell's condescending denigration of street preachers and street preaching. He makes it clear that the "bullhorn man" is not reaching anyone, he's turning people off, and even Jesus doesn't like what he's doing. He goes on to say it's better to reach people by putting our arm around them, showing that we love them, showing tolerance, etc. etc.

I cut my teeth on street witnessing growing up as a baby Christian. The apostles were street preachers. One of my spiritual heroes and mentors, Rev. Glenn Adkins, has been street preaching most of his life, and as his one-time protégé and disciple, I know the power that is there when you take the Gospel to the streets. It was disturbing to hear Mr. Bell implying that street preaching or "witnessing" will make you uncool and even unchristian, just like the humiliating caricature of the "bullhorn man" he showed in his DVD.

The fact is, most Christian kids don't evangelize - at all. They don't share their faith - at all. I realized that if this DVD was shown in youth groups, they never would, because Mr. Bell tells them it is uncool and unchristian to evangelize. I knew I did not want that DVD, or any other of Mr. Bell's DVD's, shown in our youth group.

As time went by, I began to accumulate information about this young man that *Christianity Today* was calling "The Mystical Billy Graham."[1] He is pastor of one of the largest Emergent Churches in America, Mars Hill, made up of mostly young people, almost 15,000 in attendance. Bell is the author of *Velvet Elvis*, a book that is on the bookshelf of almost every youth pastor I know. A graduate of Wheaton, Bell was taken by surprise by the explosive growth in his church numbers. His second book, *The Sex God*, has also become a mega-seller.

The influence that Mr. Bell has on youth and college age kids is phenomenal. He is a pivotal player in the Emergent Church. He is a charismatic speaker, a creative teacher, and seems to be a genuinely sincere and nice person. But, again, being sincere and nice, or being a charismatic, creative speaker, has nothing to do with the truth. Because of the tremendous impact Mr. Bell is having on youth, it is our responsibility to look at what he is teaching.

My initial visceral spiritual aversion to Mr. Bell's *Nooma* DVD and the spiritual discernment that "something's not right" was soon verified for me when a new *Nooma* DVD was released called, "Breathe."

This coincided very closely, coincidentally, with another DVD release promoting contemplative spirituality called, *Be Still*. Interspersed with commentary from major Christian celebrities like Max Lucado and Beth Moore, as well as more new-age leaning people like Dallas Willard and Richard Foster, the DVD moves Christians toward "Contemplative Prayer" and learning the value of silence.

I understand the need for times of silence before God. We are too busy, and the world is too noisy. "The Lord is in His holy temple; let all the earth keep silence before Him." (Habakkuk 2:20) How can we expect to hear His voice when we never take the time to wait to hear? Silence has its place.

Unfortunately, the new push toward silence and Contemplative Prayer as it is being taught today has more to do with Hindu and Buddhist style meditation and guided visualization than any Biblical template for meditation or waiting on God. It adds "breath prayers," repetitive prayers and emptying your mind. But the only way to wait and be silent safely in this age of deceptive demonic voices is to do so with the Word of God in your lap, filling your mind with truth from it.

The DVD *Be Still* is based on the scripture, "Be still and know that I am God." (Psalm 46:10) It's a great verse, but in this DVD, the verse is taken completely out of context. If you look at this verse in context, God was not saying, "Be quiet and listen to me," but rather, "Stand still and watch me deal with your enemies." Context is everything.

Why is that distinction important here? Quite simply because the "Be Still" verse is one of the favorite verses of the New Age movement and New Age practitioners. To your average Christian, this verse means, "Be still and know God is in control." But for New Age believers, it means, "Be still and know that *I* (point to yourself) am God."

Let that sink in for a moment. That is why context is important.

As I've outlined previously, leaders of the Luciferian New Age agenda have made it clear how important it was for them to change the doctrine of the church to New Age doctrine, one doctrine at a time. By pushing occult and New Age practices such as breathing properly, meditation and silence in order to "hear the divine voice of God" packaged as a Christian experience for the hungry heart - with one single out of context scripture to base it on - they have, through marketing designed to reach unwitting and Biblically weak Christians, managed to make occult and eastern religious practices acceptable, desirable, and a way to hear God. The line between east and west has started to disappear, and other voices and other extra-biblical teachings and philosophies are beginning to be incorporated with scripture, and the One World religion is closer to reality. Those who have opened these doors through Contemplative Prayer, breath prayers and eastern-style meditation do not have any idea how dangerous it all is, and how it has opened up a whole generation of new believers to occultic, demonic influence disguised as a legitimate Christian practice. The results will be, indeed already are, devastating, as it has served to move the church completely away from Biblical practices into an experience-based way of life that does not have the Bible as the solid standard by which we "prove all things."

During the release of *Breathe* and *Be Still*, I happened upon a recording of a message by Mr. Bell, apparently given at his church, Mars Hill. [2]

I need to stop here and talk about the name of the church. I understand why he may have used the name "Mars Hill." Paul preached a sermon in a place by that name. Before Mr. Bell came on the scene, a very intellectual and sophisticated magazine was published called *Mars Hill*. I assume the idea is, Paul took a secular God (The Unknown God) and tried to use it to show that it was the God of the Christians - the Unknown God. It is not clear whether that mission outreach was successful. Even so, I understand the need to "contextualize" the Gospel in a form that the local culture will grasp.

But that is a far cry from naming your church after a Pagan god. It would be like an Old Testament Hebrew assembly calling itself "Baal Congregation" or "Ashteroth Hill Assembly." God judged His people *severely* for associating His temple or His people with Pagan gods. At the least, it shows a complete ignorance of the dangers of the demonic on the part of Mr. Bell. At worst, it may actually be creating open doors to deception. After all, if you call them, they *will* come. That is what is called "invoking" in the world of magick.

Now to return to Mr. Bell's teaching on breathing. Here is a direct quote:

> **In Yoga, one of the central tenets of Yoga, is your breath needs to remain the same, regardless of the pose... the Yoga masters say, 'This is how it is when you follow Jesus and surrender to God...' That's integrating the divine into the daily.**[3]

If you are not alarmed by that statement, you simply do not understand the danger and potent destructive power of Yoga, and of occult practices.

Why in the world would we as believers take our cues from "Yoga Masters" on how to follow Jesus? What Yoga masters is Bell referring to? Is this not a clear indication of Mr. Bell's fundamental and foundational compromise with a Pagan belief system? And if that is not clear to you, then you do not grasp how seriously God takes our opening the door to dangerous and occultic practices.

Concerned, I wrote to the customer relations head of one of the major Christian bookstores that were carrying his newly released *Nooma* DVD *Breathe*, which was a watered-down version of his *real* teachings on Yogic breathing. Here are the e-mail communications between myself and the customer relations director for that bookstore:

Dear Sir or Madam,

It has come to my attention that your stores are now going to carry Rob Bell's *Nooma* DVD, "Breathe."

You should know that Bell is now teaching an eastern-style Yoga breath technique and knows it. This is a direct quote from one of his sessions: [I had included the quote concerning Yogic breathing by Bell here – g.r.]

I am extremely concerned that you are carrying a product by someone who is taking his cues on how we should follow Jesus from "Yoga masters" - and I assure you, he's not referring to Christians. I came out of the occult through great hardship, and I am deeply alarmed that you would carry something that has the potential to lead many people into darkness and occultism.

I am asking that you remove Bell's products or at least this "Breathe" product from your stores. To not do so would lead me to believe you do not care about the Christian content of your store materials, and would make me consider not just ceasing to patronize your store, but to encourage others to do so. Your response in this matter is greatly appreciated.[4]

I admit that this e mail was deliberately provocative. I am so used to getting vague answers from people who are in charge that I wanted to provoke a response that would tell me, hopefully, where they really stood.

The response from their Public Relations department:

Dr. Reid,

After reviewing your e-mail and reviewing the *Nooma "Breathe"* by Rob Bell I find no correlation between what Mr. Bell was communicating and the subject of Yoga. He never even uses the word Yoga, nor does he talk about how to breathe. The entire DVD is a monologue about God providing breath to every living being. And, the deeper spiritual meaning of the breath He provides. He states, `You are a sacred creation of God. The divine breath is flowing through you, and it's flowing through the person next to you and it's flowing through the person next to them. You are on holy ground. There is holiness to the people around us and how you treat them. Jesus said whatever you do for them, you've done for him.

I have also discussed the DVD with our buyers of this product. Three different individuals in this area of our company had previewed this DVD prior to releasing it. And all of these individuals were shocked by the statements in your e-mail. We would have to respectfully disagree with your comments. It would appear that you have criticized this project without personally reviewing the content.

We are pleased to be able to offer the NOOMA product and the title "Breathe" is a quality product that we feel will draw the viewer into a deeper relationship with God. We will have to decline your request to have this product removed from our stores.[5]

My reply:

Dear Sir,

Thank you for your response. I am glad that you made it clear where you all stand and that you chose to completely disregard my concerns and my direct quotes concerning Bell's affinity for the "Yoga masters." I believe the desired response for me would have been, "We did some research, we found out Rob Bell is teaching a form of occult meditation breath technique and he does quote 'Yoga masters' as experts on following Jesus. We love truth more than anything so we're going to err on the side of caution and remove Mr. Bell's materials until we are confident he is not teaching unbiblical principles either on his videos or at his church."

It is very clear that you have no knowledge of the occult and eastern Buddhist/Hindu practices and its dangers, and you are completely unable or unwilling to even look at that and its influence in the Christian marketplace.

As you are "pleased" to offer Bell's products because of its quality, I will be saddened to make it clear to everyone I can that (your stores) are carrying products by someone who is promoting eastern Yoga in his personal "ministry." I deeply regret your decision, and the steps I am going to take. But if those who can take a stand refuse to, please do not be surprised if those of us who have been through the kinds of hell the occult and eastern religions produce WILL.

Regretfully,
Gregory Reid[6]

His reply:

Mr. Reid,

That is certainly a Christ-like attitude. I trust you are also perpetrating this hate campaign with other Christian retailers as well.

As I have found that most major Christian retail outlets gladly carry Rob Bell's products and that the product is well-received by a wide variety of Christians nationwide. Again, before you tear something down, perhaps having direct knowledge of it would be a good idea. View the DVD then if you disagree perhaps a better avenue of expressing your dissatisfaction would be to contact www.nooma.com.[7]

My reply:

Sir,

Being Christ-like is loving the truth that Jesus said He IS above all else. This is not a hate campaign. This is about pleading with those responsible for dispensing truth to be responsible to the truth found in the Word of God. If you truly loved the truth you would have investigated my concerns, and you have not. Attacking me with crass snippets like "that certainly is a Christ-like attitude" and accusing me of perpetrating a hate campaign does not change the heart of the issue: IF Rob Bell is truly supporting Yoga and "Yoga Masters" (Hindu and Buddhist, because a Christian "Yoga master" is not at issue) then, by supporting his product, you are enabling him in his CHURCH TEACHINGS to propagate occult eastern practices. Of course, it is entirely possible that you do not VIEW Yoga as occultic. In that case, I truly have wasted my time, and yours. But rest assured, Bell may be teaching something apparently innocent on the DVD - but it will lead people to what he really teaches, and that is clearly Biblically-forbidden occult collusion. [8]

His reply:

Dr. Reid,

The heart of the issue is that you are attacking a man of God, because he teaches in a way different than you are used to. If you can live with that. Fine. But as far as this communication string. I will no longer participate. I trust you will prayerfully consider these attacks against Rev Bell. If you are a follower of Christ that shouldn't be too much to ask.[9]

This is a stunning example of "don't confuse me with facts" that unfortunately is so prevalent in people's reactions to attempts to simply point out obvious scriptural problems with these New Age "Christian" teachings. There is no concern, no willingness to consider the facts, no considering the possibility that a well-loved Christian leader might be teaching error and occult lies.

Sincere and nice though he may be, Bell is leading thousands of young people and others in a dangerous and deceptive path, and not one major Christian leader has raised the alarm. We're afraid to "name names." I cannot be. I am more concerned for youth that God has given us responsibility to shepherd than I am concerned about a misguided pastor.

Perhaps it is that the apple did not fall far from Mr. Bell's theological tree. One of Mr. Bell's spiritual role models is Marcus Borg, author of *The God We Never Knew*.[10] In his own words, Mr. Borg says:

"I learned from my professors and the readings they assigned that Jesus almost certainly was not born of a virgin, did not think of himself as the son of God, and did not see his purpose as dying for the sins of the world ... by the time I was thirty, like Humpty Dumpty, my childhood faith had fallen into pieces. My life has since led to a quite different understanding of what the Christian tradition says about God."[11] No doubt.

Borg, a member of the apostate "Jesus Seminar" group, also, according to Professor John Malan of Middleburg, South Africa, said during his visit to South Africa that "there was never a full tomb, let alone an empty one," and added, "I think it is quite possible that his body was eaten by dogs."[12]

He goes on to say, "I learned the use of mantras [Hindu Yoga word repetition] as a means of giving the mind something to focus and refocus on as it sinks into silence."[13] It should not be difficult to connect the dots here. Rob Bell's spiritual inclinations flow straight from his own spiritual role model, Marcus Borg.

It is no surprise, then, when *Christianity Today* stated that "The Bells started questioning their assumptions about the Bible itself 'discovering the Bible as a human product,' as Rob puts it, rather than the product of divine fiat."[14] (Borg says, in *The God We Never Knew*, "I let go of the notion that the Bible is a divine product. I learned that it is a human cultural product, the product of two ancient communities, biblical Israel and early Christianity. As such, it contained their understandings and affirmations, not statements coming directly or somewhat directly from God.... I realized that whatever 'divine revelation' and the 'inspiration of the Bible' meant (if they meant anything), they did not mean that the Bible was a divine product with divine authority." And, "Jesus almost certainly was not born of a virgin, did not think of himself as the Son of God, and did not see his purpose as dying for the sins of the world."[15]

No surprise, then, that Mars Hill's website speaks of the Bible as the "voices of those who came before us" - not as God's Word:

> **We believe the Bible to be the voices of many who have come before us, inspired by God to pass along their poems, stories, accounts, and letters of response and relationship with each other and the living God. These words have been used to describe God and his character for thousands of years, and we call this theology. Theology is one of the best ways we can come to know and love God; it is also how we understand who God calls us to be and what he calls us to do. Theology comes from the Greek**

94

words "theos" and "logos." Theos means God, and logos means word. Words about God.[16]

You can see how Bell's theology mirrors Borg's almost precisely, right down to the "Bible as human product" to "What if Jesus wasn't born of a virgin?" nonsense in *Velvet Elvis*.[17] On page 180 and 184 of *Velvet Elvis*, Bell expresses his high opinion of Borg's thinking. But then, Bell also recommends to young minds that they take three months off to read Ken Wilber's *A Brief History of Everything* to have a "mind blowing introduction to emergence theory and divine creativity."[18] And Wilber, according to researcher Roger Oakland, was:

> ...raised in a conservative Christian church, but at some point he left that faith and is now a major proponent of Buddhist mysticism. His book that Bell recommends, *A Brief History of Everything*, is published by *Shambhala Publications*, named after the term, which in Buddhism means the mystical abode of spirit beings. Wilber is one of the most respected and highly regarded theoreticians in the New Age movement today. Wilber is perhaps best known for what he calls integral theory. On his website, he has a chart called the Integral Life Practice Matrix, which lists several activities one can practice 'to authentically exercise all aspects or dimensions of your own being-in-the-world.' Here are a few of these spiritual activities that Wilber promotes: Yoga, Zen, centering prayer, kabbalah (Jewish mysticism), TM, tantra (Hindu-based sexuality), and kundalini yoga. There are others of this nature, as well. *A Brief History of Everything* discusses these practices (in a favorable light) as well."[19]

Shouldn't we be more than a little nervous that Bell is recommending that people read Wilber's clearly occultic materials?

Now, if your concept of the Bible is a book of collective stories, the product of two cultures telling their stories, the voices of those who have gone before us, and that is all, there is no point in you reading further. Clearly, the Bible is not God's "breathed" Word to you.

But if you *do* believe that the Bible is the inspired, God-breathed, powerful Word of God, why are you not alarmed that someone with such a weak and false view of the scriptures is so highly exalted in the Western church world? The fact that Mr. Bell does *not* believe the Bible is the infallible Word of God is enough for me to thoroughly divest myself of all things Bell. I am sorry for him. But we should not allow his misguided spiritual perception to become acceptable in the church which is mandated to be the guardian of truth.

Before Christians continue to promote Rob Bell and his books and DVD's, it is important that they look at what he actually teaches. The following quotes are from *Velvet Elvis*.

> **The Christian faith is filled with change and growth and transformation. Jesus took part in the process, by calling people to rethink faith and the Bible and hope and love and everything else.[20]**

There is *so* much wrong with this idea. Jesus certainly did not "take part" in the process of calling people to "rethink faith and the Bible." He clarified what was *already there* in the scriptures that others had distorted. Bell makes it sound like Jesus took part in transforming the "Christian faith." No. He *authored truth*. And He *was* the truth. Transformation comes from receiving truth, not "rethinking" it.

Jesus didn't call people to "rethink the Bible." He called them to strip the scriptures of all the additions and subtractions of man, and believe what *God* had said!

> **You will find yourself living more in tune with ultimate reality, you are more and more in sync with how the universe works at its deepest levels.[21]**

That is New Age confusing "newspeak" at its deepest. This statement could go straight into a New Age Journal without editing, and it would not be rejected. What is "in tune with the ultimate reality"?

What is "in sync with the universe as it is at its deepest levels"? This is the sound of depth, signifying nothing. Oprah Winfrey speaks of "the universe" but she speaks as if it is a person. It is not. It is a thing. God is a person. We can only be "in sync" with Him, His will, His plan for us.

> **"Jesus at one point claimed to be the way and the life. Jesus was not making claims about one religion being better than other religions."[22]**

Yes, actually, He was. But more than that - and it is astonishing Bell doesn't get this - Jesus said, "No one comes to the Father, except by Me." (John 14:6)

Bell falls into the classic error of someone who is disposed to error - he only quotes part of a verse or passage. He quotes the "I am the way" part but leaves out entirely the "No one comes to the Father but by Me" part. And half-quotes are the breeding ground of the enemy's world of spiritual deception. The part Bell left out not only claims the superiority of His Way, but the *exclusivity* of His way. Jesus made it clear that He Himself *is* the way. Not Buddha, not Krishna, not any other "religion" or "way." It is more than a little disturbing that Bell excised this last part, for it is the basis of our confidence in telling people Jesus alone can save them from eternal death. Without that, we're *just* like every other religion.

Bell implies that by Christians saying that Christianity is the only way to God, they are missing it. I agree. *Jesus* is the only way to God, not Christianity. I have serious doubts that Bell would agree. Someone needs to ask him if he does. Bell continues:

> **Rather, He was telling those who were following him that his way is the way to the depth of reality.[23]**

I don't even know what he's talking about. What is the "way to the depth of reality?" Bell says:

> **This kind of life he was living [implying that he was just a human living life, not God come with a mission**

– g.r.] perfectly in connection and cooperation with God, is the best possible way to live. It is the way things are.[24]

Am I missing a translation gene here? "It is the way things are." What things? "The best possible way to live"? Is that what Jesus came for? "Better living and more depth"? Jesus came to *die*. He said, "Now is my soul troubled; and what shall I say? Father, save me from this hour: but for this cause came I unto this hour." (John 12:27) That was his mission, not to give us a nicer way of life. His *central* mission was to be crucified and rise again, and everything else comes from His blood sacrifice. He Himself is the source, the word, the truth, *all*. Not "the best possible way to live."

In one portion of *Velvet Elvis* called "Springs," Bell uses an analogy of the springs of a trampoline to describe truth: it stretches, it flexes. This is where Bell's true view of scripture becomes very evident:

Once again, the springs aren't God. They have emerged over time as people have discussed and studied and experienced and reflected on their growing understanding of who God is." [25]

What a shallow, humanistic view of truth that is, and how far from the Biblical understanding that truth was about a Holy God speaking to men, and them scribing what He said to them. "For the prophecy came not in old time by the will of man: but holy men of God spake as they were moved by the Holy Ghost." (2 Peter 1:21) True or not? "All scripture is given by inspiration of God, and is profitable for doctrine, for reproof, for correction, for instruction in righteousness." (2 Timothy 3:16) True or not? If true, then scripture, old and new, is the product of God intervening and moving upon men to transcribe His heart and mind to them, not people sitting around in round table forums figuring out what truth is, as if it were a college discussion group. The truth is *not* a spring. The scriptures are not a spring that grows and expands and emerges over time as we discuss them. *We* grow in our understanding of truth, but truth is not mutating and conforming to fit our finite minds and our corrupt cultures. Truth is what it is.

Bell continues:

> **Our words aren't absolutes. Only God is absolute, and God has no intention of sharing this absoluteness with anything, especially words that people have come up with to talk about him.**[26]

This is so subtle; you will miss the implication of what he is saying if you do not understand Bell's real meaning and his real theology. Bell, being a devotee of Marcus Borg, has abandoned a faith in God's word as absolute truth and authority, and has come to believe the Bible is not the result of divine fiat but a human product. In other words, for him, the Bible is just stories, people trying to figure out this God thing. When he says "our words aren't absolutes" he appears to mean, "The Bible's words aren't absolutes because men wrote them." But Jesus said, "Heaven and earth will pass away, but My words shall not pass away." (Matthew 24:35) True or not? *Our* words may not be absolutes, but *God's* Word is. The Psalmist said, "Thou hast magnified thy word above all thy name." (Psalm 138:2) That's pretty serious, is it not? Jesus frequently quoted and attested to the absoluteness of the Old Testament. Bell just sees "stories." Bell says elsewhere, "God has spoken and everything else is just commentary." I fear he may mean the *Bible* is all commentary; because either the Bible is God's Word or it is not, and then that *is* the truth, or the Bible is the commentary and whatever Bell thinks is "God spoken" is what matters, but he never makes clear what that *is*. Which leaves everyone else as confused on the matter as he may be. My question for him is, when and where, then, did God speak? And if the Bible is all stories, which if any part did He speak? And who is to decide such a thing? If you pick and choose which parts of the scripture you think God spoke, then your view of truth isn't a spring, but a trap. It just becomes "your truth, my truth" and *nothing* is sure, *nothing* is reliable, *nothing* is absolute.

When Bell says God has no intention of sharing His absoluteness with anything, I fear he means God didn't intend to share His absoluteness with the book we call the Bible - otherwise he would have said he won't share it with any*one*. Bell frequently quotes Rabbis and Jewish scholars of old. But apparently he has little respect for their sacred understanding of the text of God, for they considered the scriptures so holy and so absolute that if a scribe were copying it and had nearly finished and made *one tiny error* of any kind, the whole manuscript would be thrown out and they would have to start again. That is a *far* cry from the liberal and uncertain view Bell has of the Word of God.

Bell goes on to point out what he considers to be the danger of the "brick wall" concept of truth, putting forth the idea that:

> **If you found out Jesus had an earthly father named Larry, they find Larry's tomb, do DNA samples and prove beyond a shadow of a doubt that the virgin birth was really just a bit of mythologizing the Gospel writers threw in to appeal to the followers of the Mithra and Dionysian religious cults ... what if that spring were seriously questioned? Could a person keep jumping? [He likened truth to the springs of a trampoline, thus the "jumping" analogy - g.r.] Could a person still love God? Could you still be a Christian? Is the way of Jesus still the best possible way to live? Or does the whole thing just "fall apart? [27]**

In a word, Rob, yes. If Jesus had an earthly father then He deluded himself by saying He was from above and the only begotten son of God who could say, "Before Abraham was, I AM." Then he cannot be trusted at all, and if the Gospel writers put in the virgin birth as a bit of mythologizing to appeal to Pagans, then the Gospels are lies and exaggerations and we shouldn't believe any of it because you don't follow truth put forth by liars and exaggerators. And then, yes, the whole thing falls apart, and you could keep jumping, but you will be absorbed by the New Age Religion as you do because you are no longer following the real Jesus or the real Gospel. You could still believe you loved God, but you wouldn't really have a clue who He *is*, because now you'd be doubting everything Jesus said, or even if he said it or the apostles made it all up. And no, you couldn't still be a Christian because by definition a Christian is committed to the truth of what Jesus said and who He was, and if you doubt what is written, it is no longer being a Christian, it's just your own hodgepodge opinion and "rubber tree plant hot apple pie in the sky hopes" religion. So yes, Rob, it would fall apart, as well it should. But Jesus' dad wasn't Larry, no DNA has been found, and atheist drivel about Jesus' birth being a take on the Mithras myth is a lie. But unfortunately, your words have succeeded in putting seeds of doubt in the minds of all your young readers, who never heard of Mithras, but will sure enough Google it now that you mentioned it. And there are plenty of lies to screw up their minds on it from the devil's sewer out there.

The fact is that if you tamper with truth - the virgin birth, Jesus as God's only begotten son, etc., then, no - the "way of Jesus" is not the best possible way to live, because you don't even know if it's real anymore. Jesus didn't say He came to show us "the best possible way to live" anyway. He said He came to die as the sacrificial lamb for man's sins. "For this cause I came into the world." Jesus is not Gandhi. He didn't come to teach us to be social revolutionaries, or even nice people - He came to call us to follow Him without reservation, even to the death. You can't follow someone that might be part myth to the death and still be sane.

It becomes evident at this juncture that Bell is writing from a carnal "logismos" mind, and the "natural man," Paul said, cannot receive the things of the Spirit, because they are spiritually discerned. (1 Corinthians 2:14) I think Mr. Bell must have been gravely wounded in his theology classes, and his faith so shattered that he had to come up with an alternative faith in which you didn't *need* the Bible to be true to follow Jesus. And that makes me very sad, and it makes Mr. Bell not someone to emulate. He is confused, and lost, and letting Satan build a kingdom of springs around him.

Bell continues:

God is bigger than any wall. God is bigger than any religion. God is bigger than any worldview. God is bigger than the Christian faith.[28]

That means, I assume, that the "Christian faith" is just another flexible trampoline spring, then. Not absolute, not the only way. But Jesus *said* He was the only way. True or not? Because if the Christian faith is not it, then there are a lot more fun, a lot easier and a lot more pleasant religions to follow.

Bell continues with the trampoline analogy:

> **You rarely defend a trampoline. You invite others to jump on it with you...You rarely defend things you love.[29]**

But Jesus and His Word are not a joyride trampoline jump. He is a life or death choice. *He* said so. You don't defend a trampoline, but you *do* defend the ones you love - and the One you love - Jesus. He's not a joyride to eternity. He is the Lamb of God in Revelation. And all but one Apostle died "defending the faith," not because they invited everyone to jump with them, but because they opposed the corruption of this world and "commanded men everywhere to be saved." Truth is not a spring, but a House, solid and true, built on the Cornerstone, Jesus. I am sorry that Mr. Bell seems to be devoid of even the most basic Bible understanding of this. I pray he will one day meet the Author of the Book he has so painstakingly diminished and minimized in his book.

Mr. Bell says:

> **The problem with 'brickianity' is that walls invariably keep people out.[30]**

Jesus said, "I am the door." (John 10:9) Obviously, a door lets people in - but also keeps people out. Jesus said the way to destruction was broad, and many are those that go that way; narrow was the way that led to eternal life, and *few* that found that road. Everyone is invited; but he who did not come in through the "Door of the Sheep" was a thief. Plenty of people were going to stand before Him at the last and be rejected because they did not enter in His way. That is keeping people out, is it not? The invitation is to *all*; but few are those who enter in.

Mr. Bell says:

"[Jesus] is giving his followers the authority to make new interpretations of the Bible." [31]

But Peter said clearly, "Knowing this first, that no prophecy of the scripture is of any private interpretation, for prophecy never came by the will of man, but holy men of God spoke as they were moved by the Holy Spirit." (2 Peter 1:20-21) True or not? If true, Jesus did not give them authority - nor us - to "make new interpretations." They merely unearthed the eternal truth already and always there in the scriptures. Bell's statement gives the very dangerous impression that we can interpret the Bible as we go along. That is how cults come to be. "New revelation" is the hallmark of cults. There *is* no new revelation - just new light shone on eternal truth, already present.

Mr. Bell quotes a woman who said, "I decided to get back to the Bible and just take it for what it really says." Bell calls that view "warped and toxic."[32] Why is it warped and toxic to believe the simple truth of God's Word? Even Occam's Razor says, "All other things being equal, the simplest solution is the best." *More* warped and toxic, I believe, is to make up truth as you go along according to humanistic reasoning and cultural preferences and demands. No, we're not all going to agree about everything in the scriptures. But when we decide truth is stable and knowable and that God expressed His truth in a Book, then though we see it "through a glass, darkly" we still know we are moving toward the clarity of revealed Biblical truth. That's not toxic. That's real. I find it so insulting that Bell considers the idea of taking the Bible for what it says "warped and toxic" when it has been this same simple faith that for centuries cost believers their lives. It wasn't great spiritual theologians who could talk their way around any argument with great words of self-wisdom that spilled their blood for the faith; it was common people who did nothing more than believe the Bible, love God, and love His word with all of their hearts. I remember the story of a little Russian girl during the Soviet era, who's Bible had been thoroughly spat upon by Soviet soldiers, and how she knelt down and wiped the spit off of her Bible with her hair - before she was shot. How can Mr. Bell treat this sacred text, and those who have given their very lives just to keep a page of the scriptures hidden from their cruel persecutors with such casualness and arrogant disdain, considering those who love the Bible so simply as people whose view is "warped and toxic?" It is in fact what *he* is teaching - the disrespect and tearing down and questioning and fairy-tale-ing of the Word of God - that is not only toxic, it is *demonic*.

Bell says, lest there be any doubt of where he stands, that the scriptures "aren't first and foremost timeless truths."[33] Then what are they, Mr. Bell? Bell says you can *find* timeless truths present in the Bible because they were true in real places at real times. This implies that truth is time-bound, and therefore, changeable. But God said, "I am the Lord God, I do not change." (Malachi 3:6) And again, "Heaven and earth will pass away, but my words will not pass away." (Luke 21:33) Isn't it pretty clear that truth *is* timeless, and applicable at all times to all people in all circumstances?

Bell further states:

> **Let's make a group decision to drop once and for all the Bible-as-owner's-manual metaphor. It's terrible. It really is.**[34]

Maybe for you, Mr. Bell, but leave me out of your group decision. When I gave my life to Jesus, I was so filled with lies and occult deception and mental and spiritual illness and darkness that I was incapable of functioning in truth. The Bible became, in fact, my owner's manual, my medicine, my love letter from God, my revelation, my light and a thousand other things. You denigrate it by suggesting it is not at the *least* an owner's manual, and much more. You treat it like Aesop's fables, sir, nice stories with a nice moral to live by. And perhaps, that is all it is to you.

Mr. Bell says:

> **"The Bible has the authority it does because it contains stories about people interacting with the God who has all authority."**[35]

No, it has authority because it is, as previously stated from Peter, inspired - "God-breathed." But if you wish, you can discard Peter's words, then Paul's. Then, well, you become the sole arbiter of what is true and what is not, do you not?

Mr. Bell states that:

This is part of the problem with continually insisting that one of the absolutes of the Christian faith must be a belief that 'scripture alone' is our guide. It sounds nice, but it is not true."[36]

He states further:

When people say that all we need is the Bible, it is simply not true.[37]

Why not? It has worked quite well for centuries for millions around the world, Mr. Bell.

The more I progressed through *Velvet Elvis*, the more I realized the book is a subtle and systematic destruction of faith in the Bible as God's Word. What a terrifying task for such a young and influential person to take on. Rather than give lost youth an anchor of confidence that the Word of God can be trusted, he is unwittingly acting as an advocate for the one who said in the garden, "Did God really say..." Bell has turned his own theological doubts into a satanically motivated effort to remove the security of truth from all who read this unfortunate and highly seductive book.

Bell states:

When Jesus said, "No one comes to the Father except through Me," He was saying that his way, his words, his life is our connection to how things truly are at the deepest level of existence.[38]

Wrong. Jesus was saying, "No one can belong to God except through Me." You go through Jesus, the one who gave His blood as atonement, or you *don't* get to the Father. I am totally amazed at how

Mr. Bell reinterpreted Jesus' words to strip it of *all* truth. And so it goes throughout the entire book.

I believe I may have gotten some insight into how Rob Bell became a prophet of distortion. On page 104 of *Velvet Elvis*, he speaks of being overwhelmed by his growing church and not even being sure he was a Christian anymore, didn't know if he wanted to be. Did anyone catch that? He said the room was filling up with hundreds of people, and he didn't even know if any of it was true anymore. He admitted he was exhausted, burned out, full of doubt, done. Most of us in ministry have that moment. It is the moment where we either steel our hearts and say with Paul, "Let God be true and every man be a liar" and have faith in the dark and "having not seen, believe" and abandon ourselves to His care, or... we break. We fold. We open our hearts to alternative explanations for our wounded and failing faith. I fear Mr. Bell has accepted the latter. It has happened many times before - nominal believers who, when they were tried by lies, believed the lies because it is simply easier to give into them. It is tragic when it happens, and those who have been so broken and disheartened need to be loved and restored. But when someone accepts those lies and becomes a leader of thousands of young people - that becomes a very serious matter indeed, requiring not simple compassion but a withdrawal of support and a challenging of the deceptions that are now being put forth.

Absent in Rob Bell's book - perhaps his whole theology - is any mention of the devil. I believe he was shipwrecked by an enemy he did not know, by a war he did not comprehend. Mr. Bell is a casualty of war. And by default, he has become somewhat of a spiritual Tokyo Rose, encouraging the soldiers of the Cross to give up the battle for truth and for the preciousness of the scriptures as God's Final Word and absolute truth in exchange for a joyride on the trampoline of bendable truth.

Bell's solution to the battle is:

We have to listen to what our inner voice is saying.[39]

That is a bad idea and a terribly wrong solution. (See Barbara Marx Hubbard quote at the beginning of chapter eight). Jeremiah said, The heart is deceitful above all things, and desperately wicked: Who can know it?" (Jeremiah 17:9) Mr. Bell has unwittingly become an echoing voice of the New Age: "Listen to your inner voice." No! Your "inner voice" lies and deludes. Listen to the Holy Spirit. He will give you truth, the way out of pain. Your "inner voice" will lead you to spiritual death.

Mr. Bell has a totally New Age view of man. It's called "human potential." He quotes Jesus saying to Peter, "O ye of little faith, why did you doubt?" (Matthew 14:31) and says,

Who does Peter lose faith in?
Not Jesus: Jesus is doing fine.
Peter loses faith in himself.[40]

What a horrible twisting of scripture. No, he just let his fear overcome his faith in Jesus. Bell says the thing that frustrates Jesus was when his disciples lost faith in themselves. He's frustrated because they don't realize how capable they are. This is almost identical to a quote from New Age teacher Marianne Williamson, author of *A Return to Love* and promoter of New Age channeled *A Course in Miracles*: "Our deepest fear is not that we are inadequate. Our deepest fear is that we are powerful beyond measure."[41] I hope Mr. Bell isn't reading this material and picking up some of his ideas from it.

Jesus said, "Without Me, you can do nothing." (John 15:5b) But Bell says this:

It isn't their failure that's their problem, it's their greatness. They don't realize what they are capable of. [42]

This is an astonishing extrapolation of a truth that is non-existent and non present in either the words or implications of scripture. Only New Agers teach how great *we* are. The Word of God teaches "How great *thou* art." We are just servants that "hold this treasure in earthen vessels." (2 Corinthians 4:7)

Bell says:

Shame has no place whatever in the Christian experience.[43]

He further states that:

God is not interested in shaming people; God wants people to see who they really are.[44]

At this point I am almost convinced that Mr. Bell has not really read the scriptures much at all. No, God doesn't want to humiliate us, but the Word is full of things like, "God be merciful to me a sinner!" (Luke 18:13) and to David, "'Thou art the man!" (2 Samuel 12:7) and "Woe is me, for I am a man of unclean lips and dwell in the midst of an unclean people." (Isaiah 6:5) Shame is the first step to repentance, and then deliverance and healing. God didn't tell these people, "Get up already! You don't realize how great you are!" Even the woman caught in adultery was in shame. Jesus didn't *add* to her shame. In fact he came to remove it from her. But he didn't say, "You're ok; just realize how great you are." He said, "I don't condemn you. Now go and don't sin anymore." God was always showing His people how unclean, incapable, broken and lost they were. They surrendered, and then they were healed and lifted up as a result. Without that process, they would remain just self deceived little "gods" who didn't realize their "greatness."

Bell says:

Poverty, injustice, suffering - they are all hells on earth, and as Christians, we oppose them with all our energies. Jesus told us to.[45]

I have a simple question: Where?

Bell then makes an extremely revealing statement that really sums up the New Age claiming of his spirit:

God made us in His image. And God calls us to return to our true selves. The true, whole people God originally intended us to be before we veered off course.[46]

A clearer New Age view could not have been written on man's condition. Rather than the Biblical view that man was born into sin, and born broken, Bell says we're called to "return to our true selves" as if all we needed was a simple "course correction." If that were the case, God would have sent a navigator, not a Lamb to be sacrificed for our sins. Bell's statement sounds just like *A Course in Miracles*, where it teaches that man's only sin is to fail to recognize he is one with God already - the "At-One-Ment." We do not need to return to our "true selves" - we need redemption and salvation and transformation through the blood sacrifice of Jesus, to be *born again* and to let the old man, which was corrupt, *die*. We don't need self-realization about how we're awesome and then just straighten out our course. We need repentance, brokenness, surrender to the Cross, and then God will heal us, save us, lift us up into *His* true greatness for our lives.

Bell is apparently a reconstructionist as well:

Litter and pollution are spiritual issues.[47]

No, they're issues of *human selfishness*. The true pollution Bell *never* addresses is man's corrupt heart and sinfulness outside of Jesus. Bell states that the prophets "did not talk about going somewhere else at the end of time. They talked about God coming here at the end of time." (p. 160) But there *is* a heaven, and we *are* going there. Hebrews says, "For here have we no continuing city, but we seek one to come." (Hebrews 13:14) Bell, unfortunately, shares with all New Agers the idea that we are to repair the earth and bring "heaven on earth." He has very dangerous theological companions, indeed.

In short, Mr. Bell does not believe in the need to "preach the Gospel to every creature." He is anti-evangelism, is a reconstructionist who thinks we just need to get our thinking straightened out and return to who we really are - not be born again. He does not believe the Bible is the inspired, God-breathed Word of God, he doesn't believe we're going to heaven, he never talks of hell except as a vague allegory, and he appears to think that Jesus is a good example to follow and little else. He never speaks of the battle, spiritual warfare, or the devil.

And he teaches Hindu-style meditation and breathing.

His latest book is called *The Sex God* and has a chapter called "God Wears Lipstick."

He recently teamed up with Emergent Church leader Doug Pagitt to participate in what was to them a thrilling invitation to be part of the Dalai Lama's U.N. sponsored "Seeds of Compassion" event that will "celebrate and explore the relationships, programs and tools that nurture and empower children, families and communities to be compassionate members of society..."[48] They will sit at the One World table with Muslims, Hindus, Buddhists and other major Pagan voices to discuss the future of our youth. My guess is that Bell did not share the truth of the Gospel of Jesus Christ. He would have to believe in the Gospel of the Cross to do so.

He is a perfect youth leader in a New Age world. Sadly, His Gospel is vague, powerless, nice, and harmless. And deadly.

He is just the kind of leader the spirit of the New Age is looking for to anesthetize and render useless a whole generation of lost kids.

For our youth's sake — for Rob Bell's sake — for Jesus' sake and the sake of truth — please see Rob Bell for the lost soul that he is. Stop buying his books and DVD's and stop supporting his kingdom of Springs. Pray for him. But keep his poison away from your kids.

Chapter Ten

Heaven on Earth

—ɯ—

In your wholeness all of you will heal the world and make it ready to participate in the building of the New Jerusalem.[1]
Barbara Marx Hubbard, *The Revelation*

We can reorient our great social and scientific capacities in alignment with Christ consciousness to transform this Earth from a place of pain and sorrow to a Kingdom of Heaven.[2]
Barbara Marx Hubbard, *The Revelation*

It is time that the church woke up to its true mission, which is to materialize the Kingdom of God on earth, today, here and now...People are no longer interested in a possibly heavenly state or a probable hell. They need to learn that the kingdom is here, and must express itself on earth...The way into that Kingdom is the way that Christ trod. It involves the sacrifice of the personal self for the good of the world, and the service of humanity. [3]
Alice Bailey, Theosophist and founder of *Lucifer Trust*

...a new world order was possible and coming. The prophets used many images to convey this new world

order. They spoke of new heavens, a new earth and a new
heart. A new day is coming – a new earth, a new world
order, a new realm – in short, a new kingdom. [4]

Brian McLaren, *The Secret Message of Jesus*

One thing that the Purpose-Driven movement and much of
the Seeker-Friendly movement have in common with the
Emergent Church is the growing idea that we are to create heaven on
earth. They are teaching that there is no need to prepare for eternity
(or prepare others, either) nor to look for an apocalyptic end and a
return of Jesus to redeem His people.

Instead, the new mandate is for us to repair the earth (a Kabbalistic
concept known as Tikkun) through going green, curing disease and
bringing world peace. Rick Warren, who has no problem sitting down
(as Hitler did) with the Grand Mufti of terrorist state Syria, claims
to be a member of the Council on Foreign Relations, a central One
World Order organization. Rick Warren does not preach the Gospel
that Christians around the world are dying to proclaim – no, he
wants to turn nations into "Purpose-Driven Nations." Thus you have
Rick Warren's P.E.A.C.E. Plan, which he recently altered to change
the "P" – "Planting Churches" to "Promoting Reconciliation," even
further removing the Purpose-Driven from a Biblical purpose and
further into a New Age template. His P.E.A.C.E. plan (Promote
Reconciliation, Equip Leaders, Assist the Poor, Care for the Sick,
Educate the Next Generation (nothing at all about Jesus or the
Gospel) has nothing in common with the command to "call all men
everywhere to repent" (Acts 17:30) and redeeming man from eternal
hell, but rather it is an attempt, however noble appearing, to fix the
social issues that sin and man's evil have created. He is offering only
a socialist, humanist band-aid.

Well, the world does not need a band-aid. It needs a cure. It
needs spiritual deliverance.

I believe the church *should* be invested in compassionate ministry
to the poor, the sick, the widow and the orphan – all of that and more.
And if we are truly following Jesus, we will. It is who we are.

But I am afraid that while the New World Order "repair the earth"
voices like Rick Warren, Brian McLaren, Tony Campolo, Rob Bell,

and Dan Kimball have fallen under the sway of the false illusion of being significant to the world, like "the church in shining armor," they have all but neutered the message of salvation that makes *any* of that matter.

Bluntly, if you feed a homeless person (which we should) and fail to lead them to eternal life through Jesus, that person will simply exit this life with a full stomach into eternal separation from God in hell. "For what shall it profit a man if he shall gain the whole world, and lose his own soul?" (Matthew 8:36) The "Heaven On Earth" folks have twisted the well-known quote of "Preach often, and if necessary use words," and taken it to the point where they use words to preach not at all. At least, not Bible words of salvation, sin, repentance and redemption.

It is a matter of simple priorities. History has proven that where true revival breaks out and the true unvarnished simple Gospel is preached, people come to repentance and are saved and it transforms society. Alcoholics stop drinking. Crime drops. Entire towns, cities and even nations are changed. But first must come the Gospel and true transformation of the people through repentance and surrender to the Son of God whose blood alone can heal, save and set free. Otherwise all you are doing is patching up a vessel that is doomed to sink.

Even the prophetic movement has moved somewhat into an area that concerns me in this regard. One of the popular teachings in it is "retaking the land" or "claiming territory for Jesus." I have no issue with the understanding that we are salt and light, and that we are engaged in a spiritual battle to take territory back from Satan in the lives he has enslaved. As I mentioned, when the true Gospel is preached and people surrender their lives to Jesus, it changes lives, then families, businesses, even cities. Some past revivals resulted in the closing of bars due to lack of business, a police department with nothing to do, and the emptying of jails!

Unfortunately, all of this teaching about "taking territory" is being done without any understanding of the "Big Picture" either Biblically or the Big Picture that the New Age One World system envisions for us all.

Biblical truth makes it clear that prophetic history is *going* somewhere. Jesus *is* coming again. He said He would come again and receive us unto Himself. He said, "Occupy till I come." (Luke 19:13) He spoke of a time of terrible tribulation to come, such as the world had never seen, nor would ever see again, and that His coming would shorten those days, or no flesh would be saved. (Matthew 24:22) You cannot with any spiritual discernment at all, read the book of Revelation – and all that it entails – including the most important "Behold, I come quickly," without understanding that this world is under a curse and judgment, and that the Chronos time of man is ticking down toward a conclusion. You cannot read, "But the day of the Lord will come as a thief in the night; in the which the heavens shall pass away with a great noise, and the elements shall melt with fervent heat, the earth also and the works that are therein shall be burned up" (2Pe 3:10) without understanding that we are not here to "repair the world" and have it clean and shiny for Jesus' return, but that we are rushing toward cataclysmic disaster, and that we are to be prepared for His coming at any time. In fact, the Bible warns about those who downplay His coming and act like we're just supposed to carry on like He is NOT coming: "Knowing this first, that there shall come in the last days scoffers, walking after their own lusts, and saying, Where is the promise of his coming? For since the fathers fell asleep, all things continue as they were from the beginning of the creation." (1 Peter 3:3-4) Does this not sound curiously – and ominously – like new Emergent teaching, and even Rick Warren, who teaches that Jesus told his disciples that "The details of my return are none of your business?"[5] You cannot *read* the Gospels, Daniel, Zechariah, Revelation and the Epistles and *get* that message. He said the day and hour, they could not know. But he did not teach that it was not important; He in fact made it plain that when we saw these signs, we were to look up and rejoice, for our redemption was drawing near. (Luke 21:28) Peter taught that the recognition of these signs was the imperative that would force us to ask, "Therefore, since all these things will be dissolved, what manner of persons ought you to be in holy conduct and godliness." (2 Peter 3:11) Or, knowing that *this* earth is going to melt away in fervent heat and judgment, then we must ask, as Francis Schaeffer put it so well, "How shall we then live?"

Scriptures Old and New are abundant with the clear understanding that there is an end to this present world system. Unfortunately, there has been an absence of nearly one full generation of real Biblical teaching about prophecy and the coming of Jesus (except as a "fiction series" and through occasional televangelists, or books not carried in most Christian bookstores!) Instead of reading the Word of God for these things and taking them at face value (even if you can't understand it all, most of it is pretty clear) new teachers like Brian McLaren have arisen to "reinterpret" the scriptures based on their personal world view and seminarian brainwashing that seeks to erase any real understanding of the coming of Jesus and the answer to the disciple's question, "What will be the sign of Your coming, and of the end of the world?" (Matthew 24:3)

If you really read the scriptures of prophecy as they are, there is not the slightest suggestion that Christians are going to save the world by recycling, even though recycling is a common-sense practice. And many of the "returnless believers" – those who planning on repairing the earth rather than waiting for Jesus to come back - are going green, including, of late, the Rev. Pat Robertson who made a commercial with Rev. Al Sharpton to encourage global partnership with the *Alliance for Global Protection* — an organization founded by former Vice President Al Gore. As with so many other things New Age, you have to dig a little beneath the surface to find some of the connections to the One World push, but it is always there. *Alliance for Global Protection* "partners" with various conservation efforts as well as the Girl Scouts and the *Earth Day Alliance*.[6] When you go to the *earthdaynetwork* website,[7] there are links to such Global Warming experts as Kevin Bacon, Chevy Chase, and Zach Braff. There is also a "Religious and Faith Communities Outreach" page.[8] On that page, you see a whole slate of One World affiliates, including The World Council of Churches, in partnership with various Muslim, Christian, and Jewish leaders. They boasted:

On Earth Day 2007, EDN was successful in creating 12,000 sermons and religious events through outreach to

leaders from the Jewish, Muslim, and Christian faiths. EDN created the 2007 Global Warming in the Pulpit Pledge as a way to engage national faith leaders and local clergy to deliver a sermon on climate change the weekend of Earth Day, April 20-22, or to commit to preaching a sermon on climate change one day during the year.[9]

Wow. That's a lot of power over the church, isn't it? 12,000 sermons and events on going green, and not a hint of the return of Jesus in any of it, I assure you. In addition, this alliance has created and pushed a "Global Warming in the Pulpit Pledge" for these leaders to *sign* to commit to pushing environmentalist issues in their places of worship.[10] This sounds eerily reminiscent of some of the Purpose-Driven "pledges" that churches and new members sign on to in committing to doing the "40 Days of Purpose" campaign, when Jesus said *clearly* not to take oaths. (A pledge is an oath with a nice religious twist.)

This is a perfect example of the Globalist, One World/One Church movement using the Evangelical Church as its pawn and mouth-piece. Reverend Pat Robertson, a reconstructionist, may regret his newfound affiliations, because he will find that the only thing that is being recycled is Bible truth – which is being "trash compacted" then brought back in a form and interpretation that makes it barely recognizable as scripture. And there are plenty of new Emergent teachers to reinterpret the scriptures for you. They are glad to explain away all the prophetic scriptures so you will sleep snugly at night and not even think about the possibility that God actually meant that He would judge this world and that Revelation judgment is coming to it. And in that regard, I find these Emergent teachers eerily similar to New Age Mother Barbara Marx Hubbard.

Hubbard went on a New Age quest to find out what was the reason for our existence. She began writing her thoughts. Then suddenly, she was hit with a feeling like a jolt of electricity was coursing through her, and her "voice" became "The Christ voice" that began writing *through* her. She "trance channeled" this false Jesus, and the result was *The Revelation* – a complete *reinterpretation* and *revision* of all the Bible prophecies concerning Jesus' return and coming judgment. As I have written in the chapter entitled, "Where Did the Devil Go?", in my dealings with trance-channelers and demonic spirits, they will do everything they can to convince people that there *will* be no coming judgment, that Jesus is *not* returning from heaven and that we must repair the planet. Does it not trouble anyone that the Emergent leaders are all speaking the same New Age language, the same doctrines and the same global view that every occult and New Age practitioner has taught for centuries? Do they really want to be in bed with that dragon? Because, like it or not, they not only are, but they have become their voices on the inside of the evangelical world.

Why is all this "heaven on earth" "repair the world" teaching dangerous and a trap?

First of all, it is parroting the doctrines of the New Age and the Luciferians.

I had an understanding from the very beginning of my walk that Satan –formerly known as Lucifer - did not *want* the earth destroyed. He is "the prince of this world." (John 14:30) It is, temporarily and until Jesus' return, sublet to him under the contract man made with him by disobedience in the garden.

What he does want is to create a perfect world. He wants to — and will — bring order in a time of global chaos. He will attempt to end poverty, stop all diseases, and "heal the land." He wants to usurp the place of Jesus as "prince of peace." He will come, in fact, as a "man of peace." He will enter a human vessel, and the whole world will follow him. Many will call him Christ – the Messiah – the Imam Mahdi – the Fifth Buddha – Lord Maitreya.

He wants to create the ultimate humanist utopia – without God. Except in the end, he will set himself up as God, which was his goal from before man was even created. It will be a place he wants to be perfect – the perfect delusion of "heaven on earth" – a place where he will rule and receive honor and then worship as he will appear to be "the emergence of a perfect human being who is heir to all prophets and pious men, the ultimate promise of all divine religions, the emergence of (the) last repository, the promised one, that perfect and pure human being, the one that will fill this world with justice and peace."[11] (Direct quote from Iranian president Ahmadinijad's "prayer" before the U.N., September 25th 2007.)

Lucifer in the flesh will come to bring it all together – a perfect world – without the God of heaven, without the God of the Bible, without the King of Kings and the Lamb of God and the Lion of Judah. It will be his final attempt, deluded as it is, to "be God" and realize his original dream to dethrone the God of heaven and become God over fallen mankind. Talk about vision casting.

Anyone with even a basic Kindergarten understanding of Daniel and Revelation knows that Antichrist is still to come, and Nero was not him, and the time of great tribulation (Matthew 24:21) such as the world has never seen and would never see again – is *still to come* – and the falling of Jerusalem *was not it!* It doesn't take a Bible scholar to figure out that many much worse times have come since the fall of Jerusalem – and it is very clear that the worst is yet to come. And Jesus said to be ready for it, not by repairing a dying planet but by preaching repentance and redemption to a dying world.

Even now the stage is being set. When the President of Iran stands before the U.N. and announces the world's desire for the "promised one" who will embody every religion and bring peace and justice, any baby Christian with even the slightest Bible knowledge of the prophecies understands that he was *not* announcing the coming of Jesus Christ. He was "preparing the way" for the one Christians have called Antichrist for centuries.

And perhaps what bothers me more than anything is that it is so obvious that my generation of boomer church leaders has failed *miserably* in teaching even the most basic of essential, historical Gospel Bible truths concerning salvation, who Jesus is, why He came and that He is coming again. As a young Christian fresh out of the occult world, I had no teacher, and I did not go to seminary. I just grabbed a Bible and studied every page of it. I did not see "A Thief in the Night" until later in my walk. I was not given a book to learn about "eschatology". All I did was read the Word of God and believe it, and there was no doubt in my mind that Jesus was coming back and that the world was catapulting toward that end. Years have passed, and that understanding has not changed; world historical events have only strengthened, confirmed and established that conviction based on the simple, untainted reading of the scriptures.

Unfortunately, my generation has caused a whole generation to grow up without this pillar-teaching of the scriptures, and thus we have a whole young generation that not only has no understanding of the things prophetic, but they are believing the words of a group of men who write immensely popular books to try to explain away *all* of the prophetic or reinterpret it to fit a New Age template. And now I can understand Jesus saying there would be a great falling away. It is upon us.

New Agers and Theosophists and Luciferians from Blavatsky to Bailey, from Marianne Williamson to Neale Donald Walsch *all* come with the same message: Forget all this foolish fundamentalist talk about heaven and hell. Heaven and hell are here on earth! Let's make *earth* our heaven. We must heal mother earth!

As I was finishing writing some of these thoughts, I had an astounding revelation. I remember that back in the 1980's, Earth Day and other environmentalist causes had deep and clear ties to not just the New Age, but to the Pagan community. "Gaia" was the goddess of Earth – mother earth, if you will. The Gaia concept and name began to appear in cartoons and children's books. The push to think of earth as a living entity as the Wiccans and Pagans do was very clear back then. Now I commonly hear Green Believers referring to the earth as "she." Suddenly, like a bolt, I saw the anti-Christ template for the coming One World/One Church. Remember: Satan mocks and counterfeits what God does.

The Bible speaks of Jesus as the Bridegroom, and the Church of Jesus as His Bride.

The counterfeit? Lucifer as the Bridegroom, and Gaia – "mother earth" – as his bride. What a brilliant mockery, and how disturbing to see so many believers moving in lockstep with it all without a clue as to its spiritual roots and implications.

When I hear Rick Warren, Tony Campolo, Rob Bell and dozens of other FutureChurch leaders doing nothing more than repeat the words of trance-channeled "Ascended Masters" and their New Age mouthpieces, I realize a huge segment of the Western church is being bridled and ridden like a helpless mule to "plow the earth" for the planting of Antichrist Global Domination and the elimination of the true message of Jesus. The true message is not "save the planet" but snatch the dying world out of an eternal hell – not "repair the planet" and "take the territory", but heal the brokenhearted and set the captives free.

Hebrews tells us we are pilgrims and strangers, and that here, we *have* no continuing city, but we seek one to come. (Hebrews 13:14) We are told that now "they desire a better country, that is, an heavenly: wherefore God is not ashamed to be called their God: for he hath prepared for them a city." (Hebrews 11:16) Jesus said, "My Kingdom is not of this world." (John 18:36) Can it be any clearer?

The point can be made from Genesis 1:28 that man *is* to have dominion over the earth. Unfortunately, we lost that dominion with the sin of Adam and the fall of man. That does not diminish our responsibility to be good stewards of what we have and to not be careless concerning the physical world that we live in. But the real dominion for believers is not over the physical world, but over the hearts and souls of mankind for Jesus Christ. We are not here to "take dominion" but to preach the Gospel to every creature, "and then the end shall come." There is an end, friends. Despite the good and practical elements behind environmental concerns, there is a larger agenda that is seeking to get believers to waste their spiritual energy on humanistic plans to save the planet. It is an agenda not rooted in concern for health and the future, but rather rooted in Pagan worship, pantheism and New Age religions. Believers unwittingly are playing right into the hand of the "promised one" that wants them to be totally distracted from their true call – to call all people to repentance at the foot of the cross of Jesus. This present world, the scriptures tell us, is passing away. (1 John 2:17) "And the world passes away, and the lust thereof: but he that does the will of God abides for ever." This is not a debate over recycling or the need to care for the environment. I do my best to do these things, but it's a personal preference and common sense, not a religious obeisance. If you search out the associations and religious connotations behind much of the "save the earth" movement, you may find yourself dancing in harmony with the Pagans, singing, "Imagine there's no heaven..." as the enemy laughs at how easily he suckered you into "passing things" and into spiritual uselessness disguised as "social awareness."

The world's upheaved environment is surely partly man's fault. We may *be* creating global warming. But that's not the point. According to scripture, nature *itself* is groaning, upheaving, drowning, on fire and erupting – not because of evil Western capital-ists but because of *man's sins*. It is groaning, awaiting redemption – not by going green – but through the manifestation of the sons of God, (Romans 8:19) Jesus' return and the establishment of a new heaven and a new earth under His rulership. Nature right now is rebelling against a godless world that slaughters the innocent and tramples the poor and is perverted and sick and evil and depraved, filling the earth with the blood of the innocent and child slavery and drug-murdered youth. It *wants* no "fix." Nature is trying to vomit us all off the planet because we are so corrupt! (See Leviticus 18:25) Nature wants no "home makeover" but rather a complete demolition and cleansing, and then a new heaven and a new earth that is free from sin which is the *real* pollution of mankind.

There is only one cleansing for sin: The blood of Jesus. The believer has one destiny: eternity in heaven, and a coming new heaven and new earth after cataclysmic judgment. Unbelievers have one hope: the Voice of Redemption spoken through the mouths of believers. My fear is that we appear to be tagging along behind the Luciferian Globalists like insecure children wanting to belong and feel significant and relevant in the face of this overwhelming Globalist movement, saying, "Look at us, we believe in taking care of the environment too!" rather than boldly proclaim the *Biblical* message, "Save yourselves from the wrath to come!"

Heaven on earth is the devil's idea so he can extend his lease. Well, the Landlord is about to reclaim His property, bulldoze it and start over. I do not want to be found fixing up a condemned property. I want to be about the Father's business, getting the children out of the house of Satan that is already on fire, even if the sign out front does say "Save the earth."

And if you have not read the Vial Judgments in Revelation, you don't even have the first clue about the "global warming" about to be unleashed.

"And with many other words did he testify and exhort, saying, Save yourselves from this untoward generation." Acts 2:40

Chapter Eleven

The Problem with Rick Warren

—⚊—

Others have written entire books on Rick Warren and the Purpose-Driven Movement. I hope not to duplicate those efforts here, but because so few people know some of the facts behind Rick Warren's Purpose-Driven movement, it is important to do at least a short chapter concerning him because of his role in the Globalization of the FutureChurch. *The Purpose-Driven Life* is one of the biggest sellers of all time. Before 2000, the name Rick Warren was barely known. Afterward, nearly overnight in fact, not only had Rick Warren begun, at least in the media, to replace Billy Graham as "America's Pastor,"[1] but his church growth model was being implemented in tens of thousands of churches across the nation and then worldwide.

These other books – which are vital and must reading – can go into depth as to why the Purpose-Driven movement is dangerous. (See Recommended Reading List.)

However, since so much of the coming Global FutureChurch deception parallels the teachings and model for church functioning and purposes of both Rick Warren and Purpose-Driven church growth plan, I must address these concerns. I will try to frame it in the form of questions that have been asked of me in public presentations. (Some not very nicely, as people who have bought into the convincing Purpose-Driven church program tend to be very angry and defensive when you question any of this.)

1. Rick Warren is a godly, caring man with wonderful teachings. Why are you attacking him?

    I am not. I do not question that he is a caring man, a nice and sincere man. But again, sincerity and niceness are irrelevant to the truth. I will, and as believers we must, question anyone who, knowingly or unknowingly, is taking the church down a path that will place it in spiritual harm's way.

2. *The Purpose-Driven Life* is a wonderful book. It's helped millions!

    I do not doubt that portions of it have helped people. The question needs to be, how, and what will be the long-term results? Is it helping people live a godlier, sanctified life free of the world, cleansed daily from sin, devoted to evangelizing the world for Jesus, lifting up the cross and the Crucified One who calls all men to repentance, and expecting and preparing for His return? An honest appraisal of those specific questions may possibly end up being, "No." Does it help people understand some basics? Perhaps. Does it help people be kinder, nicer, more tending toward the spiritual quest? Perhaps. But then, that describes Marianne Williamson's book, *A Return to Love*.

    The Purpose-Driven Life is significant more for what it does *not* teach and does *not* say than what it does. One with a strong Biblical knowledge could almost surmise that careful steps were taken to sanitize everything that even remotely smacked of fundamental Christianity in order not to scare people off or offend them or challenge them. To call it "Christianity lite" would be much more than a clever expression to get your attention. It is a diluted message. It is a weak message. It is a message that has no power to save or transform.

    Let me share my own experience with it. I read *The Purpose-Driven Life*, and I read it with no agenda. I had heard it was a great program and was told that I needed to read it. But when I finished it, my first thought was, "Why didn't everybody get these very basic principles in their first *month* of being a believer?" My second thought was, "Why were believers who had been Christians for decades so thrilled with it?" It was, at best, so elemental as to be almost shallow. There was nothing in the book that I could see that had the power to generate the kind of wild-eyed enthusiasm that readers seemed to have for it. The enthusiasm I was witnessing was more a football-rally, Amway convention type of stimulated emotional excitement than a real spiritual touch from God.

But, what bothered me most was the lack of real emphasis on life-changing Biblical principles – the Cross, primarily, but also blood redemption, Jesus' return, spiritual warfare or the power of the Holy Spirit. References to these things were minimal at best.

Also, new concepts with occult overtones were casually put in, like "breath prayers," one of the new/old occult techniques that have opened up a whole new avenue for Yogic occultism in the church.

I was especially disturbed by the deliberate elimination of the *King James* Bible, in favor of a lot of other versions, including the exotic and dangerous paraphrase *The Message* which has become *the* Bible for Seeker-Friendly and Purpose-Driven pastors, as well as the *New Century Version*, which has made the Bible practically unrecognizable from the Authorized *King James* Text because they have taken out and altered so much of it. I know that some portions of *The Purpose-Driven Life* have been instructive to some baby believers who know next to nothing. But the foundation they are getting is so weak and so void of the essentials that I fear what people have gotten is not salvation through repentance but a Better Life through Good Ideas.

After two runs through the program, one friend summed up the problem for me when he said, "I've been through the book twice. I still don't know what my purpose is." It is, unfortunately, the sound of spiritual winds signifying little.

3. But doesn't the overwhelming success of the book prove that God is behind it?

Not unless you believe the overwhelming success of Harry Potter was God's doing. Zondervan published *The Purpose-Driven Life*. And to the shock of many, Zondervan is not a Christian owned company. Rupert Murdoch, multi-millionaire, owns it. And Zondervan is not set up for your spiritual well being, but to make money. That's all. What sells, sells. And what has the potential to sell because it is market-popular and socially luring, is pushed. *The Purpose Driven Life* was a book at the right place at the right time that had mass market appeal to a generation of boomers who were looking for something pain-less, fun, light and airy to read and apply to their fast-lane lives. And just like Billy Graham was rocketed to fame when news-paper magnate William Randolph Hearst sent two words to his publishers: "Puff Graham."[2] I suspect Mr. Murdoch's people implemented a similar marketing plan.

In my opinion (and it is only that) I believe *The Purpose Driven Life* succeeded because of great marketing plus being able to appeal to a culture that is not interested in a Christianity that is going to demand much from their personal lives, but something that will "accentuate the positive and eliminate the negative." *The Purpose Driven Life* did that, and more. It offered to churches a marketing plan for church growth that was all but guaranteed to succeed. Rick Warren has promoted the plan to Jewish Synagogues. It would without a doubt work if he marketed it as "Purpose-Driven Islam" because it is a *marketing plan.* If you can market Purpose-Driven to the church, then turn around and market Purpose-Driven to a Synagogue full of lost people so they can continue to be lost on a bigger scale, what does that say about the motives of he who promotes that program? I fear it says that God is not the Prime Mover of Purpose-Driven. Corporate growth techniques are at its foundation, and it would work for a Jewish Synagogue, or a Buddhist Temple, or an Islamic Mosque.

Believe me, for thousands of pastors, many in the later years of their ministries who had labored with small, struggling churches, the Purpose-Driven model was an extremely appealing plan and an idea whose time had come. Why? Because most of us who are in ministry start out with a strong vision and lofty ambitions to reach the millions for Jesus. And nobody wants to end their church ministry with a fizzle, pastoring a handful of people for low pay and little reward. The appeal of the Purpose-Driven model is obvious.

The Purpose-Driven movement bothers me on so many levels. God did not call us to success but to *faithful service*. That does not always mean big numbers or cash flow. But if we are faithful, He can grow our church, or not – it is His to do, ours to obey. *He* brings the people as we are faithful to do as He says.

It is a terrifying truth to me that I could go out tomorrow and build a mega-church overnight. Why? Because the Purpose-Driven model works, *not* because God is in it necessarily, but because it is a great marketing plan.

The thought that I could build a mega-church and make it work and not have the Holy Spirit in it, or even present, is terrifying to me. The thought that I could be deluded into thinking God was in it *because* it was big is even more terrifying.

I am not against big. But unless the LORD builds the house, they labor in vain that build it. I'd rather minister to five people God brought than one thousand that got there through spiritual multilevel pyramid marketing and were just there for something fun and wholesome to do.

4. So what's wrong with a good church growth plan?

The early church's church growth plan was to pray, obey, take care of people and preach the Gospel of Jesus Christ under the kind of Holy Spirit power that healed the sick and raised the dead. The church grew greatly, as GOD added those who were being saved. As far as I know, no large megachurch buildings resulted from all of this. However, the success rate of martyrdom for Apostles was 99%. (John alone died peacefully.)

I am troubled with the Purpose-Driven Program because Rick Warren learned all he knew about successful church growth by attending Robert Schuller's church growth seminars.[3] And they work.

Why is this a problem? Schuller, founder and pastor of the Crystal Cathedral and spiritual disciple of *The Power of Positive Thinking* pastor Norman Vincent Peale[4], has made it very clear in numerous sermons and statements and associations over the years that he is nowhere in the same ballpark of what a Bible believing evangelical Christian is. His theology is a mix of self-help psychology and New Age inclusion. His sympathies and alignments with New Age thought have been quite obvious to anyone who researches his true beliefs.[5]

In all good conscience, I could not attend a church growth institute under the pastoral hand of Robert Schuller. If the root is corrupt, so will be the fruit. It bothers me intensely that the purpose-driven model was not a product of the Holy Spirit but of a good marketing plan developed under the church of a man who does not even believe that Jesus is the only way to salvation. Rick Warren and his defenders have tried to downplay the importance of Rick Warren's training under, and association with, Schuller's Church Growth Institute. But as an old expression goes, tell me who you're with, and I'll tell you who you are. While Rick Warren has danced around the extent of his association with Schuller and done his best to distance himself from his theology, it certainly did not prevent Kay Warren from speaking at the Rethink conference at Schuller's Crystal Cathedral in early 2008, along with a grab bag of both Christian and non-Christian speakers like Larry King, Rupert Murdoch (owner of Fox News AND Zondervan and the man Rick Warren claims is under his pastorship), former president George Bush, and a host of Emergent Church leaders as well. I find it disturbingly disingenuous to on one hand wash his hands of Schuller's New Ageism, and then turn around and ride the back of the horse because it is to his world-player advantage to do so. He should either cut all ties and renounce Schuller and all his involvement with him, or stop pretending he has nothing to do with him. His associations are giving him away.

A few other issues:

- The Purpose-Driven encourages the diminishing of the cross and its symbol and place. If the cross and its redemption are not central, it is *not* the Gospel.
- All across the country, little churches have been taken over and the pastors and dissenters have been voted out or have been force retired for not "getting with the program." Isn't

there something wrong with that? Imagine the heartbreak of a pastor who has served faithfully for thirty or forty years who suddenly finds himself out to pasture because he resisted the Purpose-Driven machine. (See *The Dark Side of the Purpose Driven Church* by Noah Hutchings in the Recommended Reading list. It is a chilling account of the results of Purpose Driven when brought to bear on small churches and faithful pastors.)

-   Rick Warren has become more of a political player than a spiritual leader. It is disturbing to see him sitting down and having tea with the Grand Mufti of Syria - one of the top terrorist states in the world and sworn enemy of Israel. It is disturbing to hear him tell the media what a great example Syria is of Jews, Muslims and Christians living together in harmony.

-   I am disturbed by the fact that Rick Warren is a member of the Council on Foreign Relations.[6] Anyone familiar with the CFR knows it is the premier American Globalist One World organization. Why would a Christian be part of an organization that will so clearly tie us into the coming One World antichrist system? Is Rick Warren truly that ignorant of the coming of antichrist and a One World government, or does he simply not believe in it? Or is this a part of his plan?

As I said, there are others who have written more extensively about the dangerousness and unbiblical foundations of Rick Warren's books, philosophies and church programs, and I am just giving you a few things that will hopefully cause you to search this out for yourself. The danger of such a movement as the Purpose-Driven church is that it is carrying out a forceful and deliberate tearing down of the Biblical model of church that has stood for centuries, and in its place is pushing what is little more than a corporate diversification and growth plan that would work whether Jesus or Buddha was behind it. It is big on growth and little on depth. It is huge on programs and tiny on the Word of God. It is a program that brings people in by the thousands, but has no real plan to disciple them, teach them or love them. It is little more than Amway on spiritual steroids – all froth and enthusiasm and very little Biblical substance. Although it is too early to see what the ultimate fruit of the Purpose-Driven movement will be, I believe that it is producing a generation of church leaders who truly *are* driven – driven to succeed, driven to build, driven to get members, driven to create more programs and committees and teams and more leaders to create more leaders – but out of it all, I have seen little in the way of humble, Spirit-anointed teachers of the true Word of God. It appears to be just developing facilitators and corporate managers. God has called us to be Shepherds, not work-force managers. Purpose-Driven has created a model where God's people are not sheep to be cared for and disciples to be raised, but rather a workforce to be used for the good of the Corporation. To the extent that they fulfill that role, they are valued and appreciated. If they don't – well, let me give you Rick Warren's own words: "It's a pretty simple rule: work with those who want to work. Amazingly, a lot of leaders never learn this principle. They spend all their time trying to corral the lazy and the apathetic, instead of working with those who want to work. I call that corralling goats."[7]

Did you get that? Sheep that don't cooperate are *goats*. But what is the Biblical reference to goats? Jesus said He would separate the sheep (believers) from goats (unbelievers) on judgment day. But in Rick Warren's Purpose-Driven model, goats are the ones who don't get with the program. I cannot even express the depth of my spiritual disgust at this arrogant and condescending view of God's people, even the ones who don't help out with the numerous and numbing church projects Purpose-Driven has created. God's people are sheep to be loved and raised, not "goats" to be mocked and rejected. True shepherds are called to "serve the flock," not marginalize and cartoonize as "goats" the "lazy church workforce." America's Pastor? Not in my book, and not in any Biblical understanding of what a real pastor is.

The apostles would be weeping, and in fact no doubt are, at this travesty of religious busy work and corporate kingdom building that is being dressed up in these false garments as "working for Jesus." The Purpose-Driven Program is going to create a generation of burn-outs that will end up with all these works – but not a clue as to what it really meant, and no real fruit for the eternal kingdom – fruit that only comes through preaching the uncompromised Word of God, whether you gain or lose numbers, whether you build or cut back, whether you live or you die.

I remember a story I read some years ago that reminds me very much of what I have seen produced by Rick Warren's Purpose-Driven Movement. It was the story of a man who went to Israel to observe shepherds and sheep in order to better understand Psalm 23. One day he asked a shepherd he was with about a large group of sheep that were being quickly driven down a hill by a man with a stick. "Why is that shepherd driving those sheep?" he asked. "That man is not a shepherd," the Shepherd he was with replied. "He is taking them to the slaughterhouse."

Satan is a taskmaster. Hereby we know the Spirit of God from the spirit of the devil: the Spirit of God *leads* us. Satan *drives* us: *do* more! Reach more! Build bigger! Do big things for God! Dream Big! Get out there and hustle for Jesus! Create programs, beat the streets, do the outreaches and fundraisers, build the care groups and get more people into the program! But Jesus *leads* us beside the *still* waters. He makes us to *lay down* in green pastures. The Spirit of God causes us to rest, not be driven in some kind of spiritual frenzy accompanied by fast and frenetic music, coffee bars and half-thought out psychological self-help messages pushed off on the sheep as "sermons." I have read enough – and seen enough – of Rick Warren and his Purpose-Driven madness to know that the Spirit of God is not the "driving force" behind "America's New Pastor."

May the Good Shepherd lead us *away* from that mass crowd of sheep who are – whether they or Rick Warren realize it or not - being *driven* to the spiritual slaughterhouse of the enemy.

Chapter Twelve

Where Did The Devil Go?

—ᴍ—

B y now most Christians have heard the oft-repeated quote that says if Satan can't get you to pay too much attention to him, he will get you to ignore him altogether.

Oh, believe me – today's church is in no danger of paying too much attention to the devil.

I am an old veteran of spiritual warfare and have been very active in that field since the Jesus movement of the 1970's. A little background on that may be helpful in order for you to understand the rest of this chapter.

There was no question for any of us newly saved and baptized believers that Satan and demons were real. Jesus said so, and He not only cast them out, but commanded *us* to do the same. We would have laughed at the suggestion that Satan and his demons weren't real, or that it was all just some symbolic "corporate and cosmic, transpersonal evil" as Emergent Church leader Brian McLaren tries to tell us in *The Secret Message of Jesus*.[1] Jesus said it, we believed it, and that settled it. It was that simple.

It was easier for me personally to understand and walk in that world than others, because I grew up practicing the occult and I *knew* the "spirit realm" was real. When I gave all of it up, I saw and experienced demons head-on when they repeatedly and visibly appeared to me in the middle of the night and tried to reclaim my life.

The first time I was asked to pray for a demonized person, I was completely untrained. There were no books, no manuals, and none of the goofy stuff that later proliferated the Christian bookstores on the subject. All of that was really to my advantage. I had to depend on God alone to teach me.

When we sat across from calm, smiling Don, he looked 100% normal. You would not have known that the day before, he had taken his little boy to the beach and carried him into the ocean in an attempt to drown both of them. Only his wife's intervention saved them. He remembered nothing of the event afterwards.

I doubted at first that he had a demon. He looked fine. But the minute we began to pray for him in the Name of Jesus, he was taken over. It was ugly. Even doors were opening and slamming as we attempted to get him free, like a scene right out of The Exorcist. God was giving me a hands-on training on how to confront and remove these ugly creatures. That was the first of what would be decades of intervention and head on confrontation with people who were demon controlled. (The Bible doesn't use the word "possessed". The word used to describe those who are taken over by demons is "demonized.")

That first experience with deliverance was at the height of the Jesus movement and Charismatic movement, and before long, "deliverance," as casting out demons was called, became a "thing." A slew of books on deliverance were written. I found most of them to be inadequate, and many were misleading, unscriptural and dangerous.

Another book could – and perhaps should – be written about true deliverance God's way (not that I have all of the answers, because 99% of it is about just being a yielded vessel and letting Jesus do the deliverance.) But my focus here is not that. I reference these things to make it clear that (1) there was, and still is, a fringe and sometimes scary and dangerous group of "deliverance ministries," (2) There are legitimate deliverance ministries, and (3) the need for those who will obey Jesus' command to cast out demons is just as important now, and perhaps more so now, than it ever has been before. At least part of the strength of my writing on these matters is precisely because I *have* engaged the enemy – in a way I pray most believers will not ever need to experience – and I have made some very clear observations that have strengthened the need for this book.

My first observation is this: Demons have identical theology. They speak as one voice in an attempt to deceive and trap people. When they control or speak through someone, as they do through the "Abraham Group" "channeled" by trance-medium Esther Hicks which became the basis for the mega-monster media occult phenomenon *The Secret* by Rhonda Byrne, they always tell the same lies, every time, with little or no deviation. This is what they say:

1. Jesus was the son of God, but not God.
2. All paths lead to God.
3. Jesus was "Christ" but we ALL have the "Christ spirit."
4. Heaven and hell are here on earth. There is no "eternal hell."
5. Jesus was just a prophet and a good man.
6. Good works are the way to reach God.
7. There are no bad people, just bad choices.
8. Stop looking for the "pie in the sky by and by." We can bring heaven here to earth by embracing all religions and all people.
9. Sin, the cross and blood sacrifice and redemption from sin are bloody, archaic man-made ideas.

The assignment of these demons, disguised as "spirits of departed loved ones" or "ascended masters" or whatever, is to deceive the hearers and to (1) Convince people that Jesus was just a good man who contained the "Christ spirit," (2) Deny the authority of the Word of God, (3) Dismiss or "reinterpret" everything about man's sin, eternal hell, Jesus' blood sacrifice, His resurrection and ascension into heaven, (4) Convince people that they can create heaven on earth through good works, and (5) Deny, ridicule, downplay or reinterpret the literal scriptures about Jesus' coming, impending judgment, the antichrist, the last days and the great tribulation.

What does this have to do with the Purpose-Driven movement, Seeker-Friendly churches and the Emergent Church movement?

I found the voices, writings and teachings in these movements to be very familiar. They are almost scripted in the uniformity of their theology. Much of what is coming out of the mouths of the teachers and leaders of these FutureChurch movements is *identical* to what I have heard spoken through demons in deliverance sessions: Don't worry about judgment. Stop talking about hell. The cross was just Jesus' way of showing man's inhumanity to man. We should embrace other religions as a way to God. Sin and repentance are old ideas that need to be replaced with good works and healing the planet.

In these new movements, Jesus has become Nice Friend, not Lord and Master. In fact, the Seeker-Friendly model urges church pastors to call him "leader" or "coach." These are ideas that New Agers will happily embrace. But they are the same ideas I have heard out of the mouth of demons trying to convince people that Jesus was just a wonderful teacher, not Lord of all and the only Son of God who died for our sins.

These new movements encourage pastors to take the cross and the pulpit off of the altar, so as "not to offend." Satan wants that. He knows, as Paul said, the cross is an *offence*. (Galatians 5:11) Satan knows it is the central message of the Gospel and the only way to salvation. He is doing everything he can to make sure it ends up in the storage closet in the church.

Emergent Church leaders talk a lot about "Following the Way of Jesus." They do not speak of surrendering to the Absolute Lordship of the Risen King, the one with eyes on fire and a sword proceeding from His mouth. Here too, New Agers are perfectly okay with those who "follow the Way of Jesus." Many New Agers *do* – or the Way of the Master, the Way of the Buddha, or whatever Way or Path they choose. It doesn't matter to them. ALL ways are correct to them. (Except for "fundamentalist" Christians and Jews, whom they consider exclusive and "haters" and in the way of bringing unity to all religions.) To them, "following the Way of Jesus" just means He's your personal role model, hero or guru. And that is exactly what demons are sent to preach and teach and encourage people to believe.

Rick Warren's Purpose-Driven model gives little importance to the last days, coming judgment and the tribulation so clearly outlined in the scriptures. Neither Seeker-Friendly nor Emergent models place much importance on any of that, and Emergent leaders like

Brian McLaren go out of their way to condescendingly downplay – or warn against as extreme -anything and everything concerning the last days or coming judgment. But Jesus said to look for the signs of his coming. (Mark 13:34-37) He said to *watch*. He said not to be unprepared. If Jesus, John, Peter and almost all of the books from Genesis to Revelation speak of and warn of and give signs about the conclusion that will surely come, then something is definitely wrong when all these voices are seeking to eliminate all talk of it, and instead present a plan to bring "heaven on earth." Edgar Cayce, the great occultist, and many others such as Alice Bailey and Barbara Marx Hubbard taught the same thing. These voices, speaking through unwitting human agents throughout the Western church now, through Purpose-Driven, Seeker-Friendly and Emergent leaders, are exactly the same as every demonic occultic voice ever uttered. Satan *wants* the church to be in complete darkness concerning these issues. Satan *wants* Christians to believe things are going to get better and better, and to believe that we are going to create a new earth.

Just like there is a growing unified voice among these movements about ignoring the last days, playing down prophecy, playing loose with Bible interpretations, working toward one-world dominionism that does not expect Jesus' return following judgment but rather repairing the planet, widening our embrace of other religions in the name of "dialogue" and "the greater good of mankind" and "getting along," this Unified Voice is beginning to resonate loud and clear with the New Age Endgame.

Emergent Church leader Brian McLaren has turned out to be a significant mouthpiece for these doctrines of demons. McLaren, a conference speaker during megachurch Willow Creek's <u>Shift</u> student ministries conference, told the young leaders that "We are in a profound shift in our world today." He also told them, "We are going through this kind of deep shift." Shift, consciousness shift, and global shift – those are all New Age concepts. Eckhart Tolle, author of *A New Earth*, wrote, "This book's main purpose is ... to bring about a shift in consciousness.... Not everyone is ready yet, but many are, and with each person who awakens, the momentum in the collective consciousness grows."[3] Again – we are beginning to hear one voice, Emergent and New Age alike. They are the Voice of the one who wishes to dominate this world without Christ in it. McLaren's stunning presentation at the Willow Creek conference, aptly named "Shift", was given without a word of concern. Bo Boshears, Willow Creek's executive director of student ministries, simply said that he does not agree with all of McLaren's views but that all youth ministers should consider his thoughts.[3]

Where did the spine of the church go? McLaren would not have lasted two minutes in our church. How can these people tolerate the spiritual molestation of our future youth ministers with the kind of New Age and antichrist theology McLaren is bringing? Where is their concern for Biblical truth? McLaren is teaching the same New Age lies you find from occult circles worldwide. He has diluted the power of the Gospel, the centrality of the cross, and the necessity of scriptural truth. McLaren, in his book *Everything Must Change*, says that the doctrine of hell needs radical rethinking, (rethinking – another New Age buzzword) that the book of Revelation does not actually teach that there will be a new heaven and a new earth, and that Jesus' sacrifice on the cross was like the Chinese student that put himself in harm's way in Tianamen square in the 1980's and that He did it to demonstrate the injustice of society that would harm a peaceful and godly man. Have the leaders of Willow Creek no integrity at all that they would allow someone who teaches these things to teach our kids? McLaren also taught that youth ministers must shift their thinking and teach teens that involvement in earthly matters is more pressing than focus on eternal matters. In addition, according to David Roach writing in Baptist Press, April 27, 2008, McLaren also said that youth ministry in the postmodern world must stop pointing to the faults of non-Christian religions, because "postmodern people do not view critiques positively." Where in the scriptures are we told that we are to stop preaching truth because it is not "viewed positively?"[4]

So in that one conference, McLaren echoed the doctrines of demons concerning hell, heaven, other religions, and the sacrifice of Jesus on the cross. At what point are we going to wake up and realize that these men are *not* preaching the Gospel but rather a demonic lie that, as Paul said, does eat like a cancer? I am stunned by those who did not have the guts to take this man right off of Willow Creek property and tell him never to return.

However, Willow Creek recently released a report in which they admitted that their years of megachurch, Seeker-Friendly methods failed to make real disciples. But what is their answer? Brian McLaren and Rob Bell? It is heartbreaking that their revelation did not lead to true repentance and a return to what is *real*, the straight-up Word of God preaching of the Gospel, but rather has become a shell game in which the last error is not corrected but replaced with a worse one.

In the FutureChurch, just as in the New Age, there is no real devil or demons but simply Lost Souls, Corporate Evil, Bad Decisions, and intentions leading to bad Karma. These new church movements are quickly becoming one FutureChurch, where there is little or no talk of the devil. There is no talk of spiritual warfare. There is no Biblical model for setting people free from demonic oppression. And in this, they are truly echoing C.S. Lewis' suggestion that you can be smack in the devil's hands by ignoring that he exists.

One of the reasons that Purpose-Driven and Emergent Churches are so attractive is because there is no *struggle* in it. Life is just a big fellowship where we do good deeds and have coffee and be nice to everybody so everybody will like Jesus, or at least not hate Him.

There is a real devil. There are real demons. And I promise you, the less they become part of our overall understanding of our Biblical walk and warfare, the more Satan will be getting into every area of our business. "Be sober. Be vigilant. For your adversary, the devil, walks about as a roaring lion, seeking whom he may devour; whom resist steadfast in the faith..."(1 Peter 5:8) If this is so, then why are these new movements so devoid of *any* teaching on this? It has all been dismissed as some vague "corporate evil."

The Word of God is very clear that there will be a time of lying signs and wonders. It also makes it clear that Satan will come as an angel of light and his servants as ministers of righteousness. The problem is that these movements hardly even acknowledge that Satan exists, much less that he is someone deserving our attention or vigilance against. If they cannot recognize Satan and his demons in their raw form, in the Biblical form, do you think they have even a small chance of recognizing them in their more "righteous" disguises, or through seemingly "righteous" people?

The devil hates the church. And he and his armies of demons all agree on the same things: In order to stop the church from being effective, they must convince Christians that Jesus is not the unique Son of God, that the Word of God cannot be totally trusted, that Jesus is not coming back in judgment at the time of tribulation and the last days, that all paths lead to God, that "all truth is God's truth," and that we must embrace and absorb other religions and ideas so we can "reach them." How do I know this? Because I have heard these same lies pouring forth out of the mouths of people who were demonized from one end of the country to the other, who did not know each other, who had no way of knowing each other. In fact, they poured out of the mouth of the medium that channeled the "spirit" of the suicided son of the famous Bishop Pike. It finally led Bishop Pike to abandon any fear that there was a real hell. He obeyed this demon that compelled him to travel to Israel to study this "new age Jesus," where he got lost in the desert and found his answer when he fell and perished in this place where he had been led by this "spirit."[5]

So when I hear the FutureChurch teachers espousing, though more subtly, the same occult lies I have heard, and once studied and believed, and read, and documented for decades out of the occult and New Age annals, what am I to say? When I hear them echoing, though not quite as directly, the same lies I have heard out of the mouths of despicable demons in the many confrontations I have had with them, what am I then to say?

I say that it appears that they are truly, to use a beloved FutureChurch phrase, "all on the same page" – demon and FutureChurch leader alike. And talk of the devil is nowhere to be found.

How better to run the show and to orchestrate the preparation of the evangelical West for the final deception and falling away, than to do it from a hidden place as the puppetmaster pulling the strings, and from a place where no one even thinks you are present, or even real?

I know exactly where the devil went. He went nowhere at all. The enemy, as Pogo said, is us, it is those unwitting mouthpieces of

Lucifer's kingdom, and the great Enemy of our souls is becoming their puppet master.

There is a war for the soul of this next generation. Winkie Pratney once wrote a book called *Devil Take the Youngest.*[6] He explained that before God was about to move among this broken world, Satan tried to destroy that move – and he did it through trying to destroy the young: the firstborn of Israel during Moses' time, the children Herod slaughtered to prevent the coming of the King, abortion, child abuse and so on.

I believe we are on the cusp of the last hour, the one that will culminate in the fulfillment of all of the Word of God, the End of Days. And I have labored with several generations of kids and washed their feet and cried and prayed that God would raise them up to be strong women and men of God who truly will change the world, who will stun the world with the power of God and the uncompromised Gospel of Jesus Christ.

Never until now have I been as heartbroken or as concerned that a generation is going to become nothing more than a group of "spiritual" kids that have no idea what it means, or where it's going, or what the true Gospel and the power of God is about. This is the generation Satan seeks to devour like a tasty morsel because he knows his time of Ascension is coming, and he wants no interference, especially from those who have the fire and the physical energy and the youthful determination to actually *do* something to interfere with his grand scheme. And so he has pulled out all the stops to anesthetize, demoralize, categorize, herd, brand and corral an entire generation of church and religious kids and a whole new crop of kids brought in through Seeker-Friendly and Contemplative and Emergent models, and make them so blind to the truth that they cannot fight, for they do not even know that they are in the middle of a spiritual war.

In twenty short years, we went from a church that was at least aware of the reality of spiritual warfare and the war we faced with Satan for the lost souls of mankind, to a church that would not recognize a demon if it showed up in full battle armor.

In this last hour, the only ones that can shatter this numbness and train up a generation who can fight for the lost of their generation and bring *true* revival are those who recognize Satan is a real foe, who know that the prince of this world is in a desperate last effort to destroy those God sent Jesus to redeem, and who are willing to go teeth to teeth with the hordes of hell and challenge them for this generation. They are willing to confront them and fight them and call out the lies of his unwitting messengers and push back the battle line that has eroded the church's defenses and caused us to slide back to the lip of hell in this last twenty years.

There is a battle underway for the truth and integrity for the Word of God, and for the very foundations of the faith we hold precious. It is a battle being waged with powers, principalities, and spiritual wickedness in high places, not with "transpersonal evil." Evil has a face. It has a name. It is Satan, and he is at war with the truth, and the church, and he is committed to shutting the mouths of all those who contend for the faith. He is committed to filling the mouths of any vessel that has thrown truth to the ground in favor of postmodern, experiential, New Age philosophy that is void of the life of Jesus that only comes through His blood. You must choose whose vessel you intend to be. All who do not serve the Lord Jesus, are by default slaves of the wicked one. This war is real, and it is fierce. Rip off the mask of the devil's lies through the Word of God and expose them for what they are, no matter what it may cost.

Chapter Thirteen

The Battle for the Bible –
Get The Message?

—ᗯ—

For truth is fallen in the street. (Isaiah 59:14b)
And an host was given him against the daily sacrifice
by reason of transgression, and it cast down the truth
to the ground; and it practised, and prospered. (Daniel
8:12)

I got my first Bible when I was fifteen and had just become a
Christian. It was called *Good News for Modern Man*. I didn't care
for it much, so on someone's recommendation, I got an *Amplified
Bible*. For years, I read that, and the *King James Version*.

Before I became a Christian, I tried very hard to read the Bible.
I didn't understand a single word. It was like reading a foreign
language. I tried time and time again. Nothing.

The day I became a believer, the Bible opened up to me like
revelation. It went from nothing making sense to everything making
sense!

What was the reason? It is because the Bible is not an ordinary
book. It is a supernatural book. It is a powerful, God-breathed text,
from Genesis to Revelation. Before I met Jesus, my spirit was dead.
My natural mind was corrupt. My heart was incapable of experiencing the Spirit of God. As Paul put it, "But the natural man receives
not the things of the Spirit of God: for they are foolishness to him:

neither can he know them, because they are spiritually discerned." (1Corinthians 2:14) "Because the carnal mind is enmity against God: for it is not subject to the law of God, neither indeed can be." (Romans 8:7) Before I knew Jesus, I was incapable of understanding the Word of God. When I gave my life to Him, the Spirit of God became my teacher, and what an adventure awaited me! I underlined every word. Within a year, the pages were falling out they had been so worn. Every book, every chapter and story gave me fresh revelation into this God who loved me and this Savior who had redeemed me from death and hell. I could not get enough. One of my fondest times in my growth was in the second year, when I worked a midnight to seven shift as a janitor. When I would get off of work, I would go home, have breakfast, and spend an hour or two just reading the scriptures and praying. I cherished those moments. They were the pivotal foundation of my life as a Christian, and that foundation remains.

I am so thankful for my early pastors and teachers, because they simply preached the Word of God and let it speak for itself. I learned from them, and from God, that the Bible doesn't need a lot of interpreting, just encouragement to apply the truth to our lives. Sure, there are things that are hard to understand. There are things I *don't* understand. And there is an unquestioned place for teachers and teaching that can dig deep from the original languages and flush out every nuance and powerful word within the Word – what Amy Carmichael called "A meadow in every flower."

I am thankful that I learned the old adage, "God said it. I believe it. That settles it." It worked powerfully in the practical walking out of my faith. I am thankful that no one got hold of me and filled my mind with a bunch of theological confusion about higher and lower criticism. I am glad I didn't have anyone fill my heart with doubts about the Bible. I just simply believed what I read, and asked God to help me walk in it. It was simple. It is *supposed* to be. In fact, Paul expressed his concern for the Corinthians that someone was complicating their walk. "But I fear, lest by any means, as the serpent beguiled Eve through his subtlety, so your minds should be corrupted from the simplicity that is in Christ." (2 Corinthians 11:3) The Gospel was not written for the brilliant, but for the child for whom the Kingdom belongs by faith. Because I learned to believe and trust the Bible this way, I am very committed to the truth and integrity found in its pages. And yes, there are debates about which translation is best. I will leave that to scholars to hash out. However, I think it would be an eye opener for believers to do an online search about the differences between the Authorized *King James* and other versions. Westcott and Hort, the two British men that developed an alternate Greek text on which most of the new translations are based, were practicing occultists that did not believe the Bible was the infallible Word of God, did not believe Jesus was the ransom for man's sins, and were part of an occult group called, "The Ghostly Guild."[1]

From their efforts to give the church a new translation other than the *King James*, they began a crack in the dam that has led this day to our current flood of translations and interpretations and paraphrases. What concerns me – and has always concerned me - is that each new version seems to take out something new, or alter something to lessen the potency of the proclamation of the Lordship of Jesus Christ.

In the last decade, I have seen a glut of Bibles hit the market like I have never seen before. History is not my strong point, but if I remember correctly, there was only one version of the Bible for centuries, and the church forbade the common people to read it. They taught that only the priesthood could correctly interpret scripture. Martin Luther came along and translated the scriptures for the common man, and the reformation was born. The authorized *King James Version* came later.

As a young believer, I read the *King James Version* and *The Amplified Bible*. I read a few others, like *The New International, Good News for Modern Man, The Revised Standard, The New American Standard*, etc., but to this day, the *only* one that burned into my spirit so deeply that I can quote almost all the verses I know is the *King James Version*. It makes me wonder about the others, really. Just from a human standpoint, almost all the other versions left me uninspired. They did not stay with me. I challenge you: If you are reading other versions, how many verses can you recite? Really? Be honest. I am not a brilliant person, and I am, as I tell my students, Bible smart and verse stupid. I can't tell you where most verses are. I really have to dig or use a concordance because I can't memorize chapter and verse information very well. But somehow, when I teach, the *Authorized King James* text flows out of me from places and books I did not even *attempt* to memorize. It makes me wonder.

I wouldn't call myself a die-hard King James Only person. But the more those new and increasingly exotic versions come out, the more I'm moving in that direction. While I cannot say I agree with everything that has been written about the KJV debate, the fact that Westcott and Hort were practicing necromancers and members of the "Ghostly Guild" and had doctrinal beliefs that were mirror images of modern New Age thought and were the ones who sought desperately to push a new translation from a questionable manuscript source to replace the *King James* makes me *very* nervous, as it should you. At the least, you should search it out.

Taking it out of the realm of that particular debate, I have long had many other concerns about the glut of Bibles out there now. First of all, Bibles are a huge money making operation. Go into any Christian bookstore and look at the vast shelves: *King James, New King James, Revised Standard, New Living, New American Standard, New Century Version, The Message.* How does one choose? Then they have burgundy, black, gold pages, leather, no gold pages with faux leather or leatherette, hardback, softback, metal covers, and embroidered covers. They have Bibles for golfers, executives, mothers, dads, kids, teens, soldiers…It is absolutely dizzying, and depressing, and confusing, and expensive. If I understand right, the only Bible that has no copyright — the only one that you can copy and print without *cost* — is the *King James.* The rest, well, they are copyrighted, and you will pay to print if you want your own specialty version.

I know this will come as a shock to many, but the major "Christian" publishers are owned by secular organizations, and they do not care about your spiritual growth. Zondervan has been owned by secular multimillionaire Rupert Murdoch's publishing conglomerate for some time. It is no surprise, really, that Zondervan is becoming the funnel of all things Purpose-Driven, Emergent and Contemplative/

Mystic these days. For these companies, it's got nothing to do with Jesus. It's what sells.

So when I see this glut of Bible translations and paraphrases, I am very concerned. The way it plays out, especially among youth is this: They will show up at a church with, say, a *King James* or a *New King James* Bible. There is a Power Point presentation in which there are *several* verses quoted. They may use several different versions for one message. What is the result? Kids are elbowing each other and saying, "That's not even close to what mine says!" Kids with discernment bristle at the contradictions. And kids with no discernment just stop bringing their Bible because what's the point? It doesn't match what's on the screen. In the FutureChurch mantra of "Everyone needs to be on the same page", *nobody* is on the same page because all the pages of *King James* have been excised and exiled to ancient status and a hundred new versions, *none* of which match, are thrown at us - supposedly to make the Bible easier to understand. But the end result is that not only are these versions harder to grasp, they are nearly impossible to retain. As a result, real Bible study has gone the way of Fundamentalist Bible Thumpers, Last Days doomsday preachers and outdated church going old folks. What we are left with is Snippet Christianity based on nice thoughts, practical words, pop psychology and a few favorite and easy to quote verses about being loving and kind and harmless. What is being created, in fact, is a spiritual tower of Babel in which everyone is been forced to speak the same language, and it has resulted in little more than spiritual babbling that makes no sense to a world that is dying and heading to eternal destruction away from Christ, and we have no power to redeem them.

I did not really understand the spiritual nature of this crisis until I was confronted with the paraphrase *The Message* by Eugene Peterson. I had first come upon it almost a decade ago when I heard a pastor use it. Always looking for a new Bible back then, I bought the only available version at the time, a Psalm and Proverbs combination. I read it. I felt very unsettled by it. Even the Living Bible fed me at times; but *this* version made me queasy. Peterson's "Bible" was tinged with terms that are more familiar to Wiccan and Pagan circles than to Christianity. I put it away, thinking that perhaps it was just me that had a problem with it.

A few years later, with the Purpose-Driven movement in full swing, *The Message* was a huge component of the program. It had also become a favorite in Seeker-Friendly churches. (In retrospect, this was probably the beginning of the Biblical Babel tower being built in our midst, as Rick Warren was very deliberate about using almost every version *but* the *King James Version* in his book, and included a number of the new and exotic translations.) Rick Warren says of this:

> **Read scripture from a newer translation. With all the wonderful translations and paraphrases available today, there is no legitimate reason for complicating the Good News with four-hundred-year-old English. Using the King Kames Version creates an unnecessary cultural barrier…Clarity is better than poetry.[2]**

But clarity based on *cloudy truth* and *questionable translations* is more harmful than having to read King James' English by far.

I decided to get a complete copy of *The Message Bible* this time. Surely, I thought, there has to be something special to this version if Rick Warren is using it! (This was before I really understood what Purpose-Driven was about and how dangerous it was.) I was kind of excited. It was leather covered, with a nice owl on the cover that said, "Think."

I started reading it again. I couldn't handle it. Something inside was just screaming. It was the same "red light" I have felt on so many occasions and with so many people and books and teachings over the years that indicated something was very wrong spiritually. But this time, I just couldn't put my finger on it.

Fast forward two years. We had already exhausted the Purpose-Driven program. I did not see any lasting fruit from it. Even the criminal who was influenced to surrender to the authorities by him being read *The Purpose-Driven Life* by a woman he had kidnapped and held captive is now a Muslim.

It wasn't until I was put in contact with a man named Warren Smith, a former New Ager, that the "red light" I was getting made sense. Warren had come out of *A Course In Miracles*,[3] among other things. *A Course in Miracles* is a set of channeled writings by a Columbia University Professor of Medical Psychology named Helen Schucman that began in 1965. (*A Course in Miracles* had been popularized and promoted by Marianne Williamson in her book *A Return to Love*[4] and promoted by Oprah Winfrey in 1992.)

Warren Smith wrote a book about his testimony and how became a Christian in 1984 called *The Light That Was Dark: From the New Age to Amazing Grace*.[5] In 2003, after reading *The Purpose-Driven Life,* Warren Smith was alarmed to discover New Age implications throughout Rick Warren's book. Warren Smith wrote a book called *Deceived On Purpose: The New Age Implications of the Purpose Driven Church*[6] to explain his concerns. It answered a number of my questions as to why the whole Purpose-Driven model was so disturbing to me. I had a long conversation with Warren, and it helped answer a lot of questions. Then we got down to my problem with *The Message*. "I just can't read it," I told him. "I just don't feel right about it." "I can show you why," Warren replied. "What does the Lord's prayer read?" he asked. "Thy will be done on earth as it is in heaven," I answered. "Now read it in The Message," he said.

I found the passage, and as I read it, my blood ran cold.

"As above, so below."

That phrase doesn't mean anything to 99% of the populous, and 99.9% of believers. But to those who know and understand the world of the occult and the New Age, it means *everything*. If you were to type the phrase "As above, so below" into a search engine, you will come up with 210,000 web site references, the overwhelming majority of which are from occult and/or New Age sites. The very first site, an occult definition site, says:

> **This phrase comes from the beginning of The Emerald Tablet [which, incidentally, is listed as the source of *The Secret* in the first pages of Rhonda Byrne's book by the same name – G.R.] and embraces the entire system of traditional and modern magic which was**

inscribed upon the tablet in cryptic wording by Hermes Trismegistus. The significance of this phrase is that it is believed to hold the key to all mysteries. All systems of magic are claimed to function by this formula. 'That which is above is the same as that which is below'... Macrocosmos is the same as microcosmos. The universe is the same as God, God is the same as man, man is the same as the cell, the cell is the same as the atom, the atom is the same as...and so on, ad infinitum.[8]

The Emerald Tablet has its roots in Egyptian priesthood and magick, and means, among other things, that God and man are equal.

There is no question that this is purely an occult phrase rooted in some of the most ancient forms of "mystery religion" teaching there is: Kabbala, Egyptian magick, Crowlyeyan magick, etc. The phrase is so clear in its meaning, that anyone that uses it deliberately must either (1) Unwittingly use it under the influence of something from the demonic realm, or (2) Knows exactly what it means.

I do not know the author of *The Message*. What I do know is that he either had to be unwittingly influenced by something other than the Holy Spirit to write something so absolutely phrase-specific to the world of ancient occultism and New Age thought, or, God forbid, he does know what it means. I can only pray it is the former. However, given Mr. Peterson's recent endorsement of an emergent-type fiction book called, *The Shack*,[8] I have to wonder.

A friend had asked me to read *The Shack*, since Eugene Peterson endorsed it. Peterson said, "This book has the potential to do for our generation what John Bunyan's *Pilgrim's Progress* did for his. It's that good!"[9]

So what is the story that Eugene Peterson thinks is on a par with that classic Christian book? It is about a man whose daughter is murdered. He gets a note from "Papa," his wife's pet name for God, telling him to meet at the shack where the tragedy happened. He goes and meets a casual Jesus, who introduces him to Papa, a big woman who cooks, and Sarayu, a girl who is supposed to be the Holy Spirit. I didn't think it could be worse until I reached the part where the man is taken before a judge whose name is Sophia – in Greek mythology, the goddess of wisdom. The New Age is rife with writings and conferences to honor Sophia. One particular New Age site ties Sophia with the Gnostics as well as Solomon's honoring of the goddess Asherah.[10] This is the new *"Pilgrim's Progress"* according to Eugene Peterson. And he is the author of *The Message*. Any questions?

An occult phrase that is *this* absolutely highly charged with occult meaning, power, and *recognition* to those in the occult world such as "As above, so below," and could pass as *scripture* and no one even notices or gives it a glance is terrifying to me. Do you understand my concern? If that were the *only* problem I had with *The Message* – and it is not – that would be enough for me to never use it again. Yet millions of people are reading it, largely due to Rick Warren's use and endorsement of it. When you really get a grasp of how far off *The Message* is, it is staggering, and I am stunned that so few Christians have seen the blatant shredding of truth done by Eugene Peterson. I can further illustrate it by giving you another example. 2 Peter 1:10 in *The Message* reads, "Don't put it off. Do it now."

But what does the *King James* read? "Therefore, brethren, be even more diligent to make your call and election sure; for if you do those things you will never stumble." There is absolutely *no* correlation between the two! It is almost like me telling a foreign audience, "Good morning, it is good to see you," and the interpreter telling them, "The sky is a brilliant color blue." *The Message* is not a translation – that much we know – but it cannot deserve to be even called a poor paraphrase. It's simply making up whatever Peterson wanted it to say, even if it didn't match even a little. Where are the Christians who study, compare and realize that this is a blatant spiritual fraud?

But beyond the issue of translations – and there are so many now it is dizzying, and I am not scholarly enough to debate the issue the way it deserves to be debated – in the prophetic sense, I see the "big picture" being just this: with each new Bible version, there are more and more portions of scripture taken out, including many references to Jesus as Lord, the blood of Christ, and many other things that make the Bible so powerful and the place and position of

Jesus so sovereign and holy. They yank it out, then add a confusing little footnote to explain which translation is added, subtracted, etc. - footnotes that do nothing but distract and confuse young believers and discourage them from just...*reading it.* Believing it. Living it. Again, it would do you well to do an online search of *King James* vs. other translations to see exactly how different some of these translations are and just how *much* has been excised. With each new version, more is taken out and changed to accommodate the times we are in and the more powerless the Word becomes. There was even a new version put together by a former Baptist minister called, *Good as New*. It was praised by the Archbishop of Canterbury, Rowan Williams, (the same that has called for England to consider establishing Sharia or Islamic laws, and who is a Druid) who called it "a book of extraordinary power."[11] According to Joseph Farah of <u>World Net Daily</u>, *Good as New* translates all demon possession as mental illness, (See chapter 12, "Where Did The Devil Go?") renames Jesus "The Complete Person" rather than the Son of Man, and has a pigeon descending on Jesus at his baptism. Matthew 26:69-70 has Peter renamed as Rocky and when asked if he was seen with "the hero of Galilee" replies, "I don't know what the hell you're talking about." 1 Corinthians 7:1-2, the passage forbidding fornication, is translated, "Some of you think the best way to cope with sex is for men and women to keep away from each other. That is more likely to lead to sexual offenses. My advice is for everyone to have a regular partner."[12] I wish I were making this up, but I am not. Yes, it is extreme, but so is the phrase from *The Message*, "As above, so below."

With each new version and each new paraphrase, less and less of what the original manuscript upon which the *King James* was translated is left intact, and more and more passages are changed, rearranged, outright removed, or retranslated to fit the moral stan-dards —or lack of them - of our day. And no one is really minding the store anymore, since most of the major Christian book and Bible publishers are secularly owned. As such, they are under the control of both the dollar and the Luciferian spirit of the age. It is a spirit that hates Jesus Christ and will do everything in its worldly and spiritual power to destroy the foundations of truth that the scriptures have laid out so clearly for the believer for thousands of years, from the Old Testament to the New. Only in the last two centuries has the Evil One been able to get such absolute reign over who reads what, and he has "puffed" and pushed those books and those translations which are the farthest away from the original manuscripts that are most reliable.

And the Evil One is not done yet. I have seen clearly that the next series of translations and "paraphrases" (90% of new believers and churchgoers don't even know the difference between the two) are going to push the envelope even further. Before long, they will publish a Bible that anyone – Buddhist, Hindu, Wiccan or Pagan – will feel perfectly at home with. It will have eliminated or retranslated most of what offends or that which makes the truth of God's Word and the Lordship of Jesus Christ so powerful. It will be the perfect New Age translation (or paraphrase) for the coming New Age and One World Religion — the FutureChurch version —that they must have to completely absorb the apostate Western church, which has begun to abandon truth for the lie. You have been forewarned. I am not calling for a total return to *King James* only, which will not please some who wish me to go in that direction. But I *am* convinced that the glut of translations, paraphrases and varieties of Bibles, each year becoming less Bible and more commentary and helpful hints for living, are taking us further and further away from being the People of the Book. God has called us to be people who know, and can quote and use with power the written Word of God - with the Spirit of God - a people who will bring the Power of God that only comes through a clear, distinct, and bold proclamation of the truth of that Word. It is a truth that calls all men to repent and to turn away from their dumb idols and turn to the Living God and receive salvation and forgiveness and eternal life through the *only way* God made available – the blood sacrifice of His Son Jesus Christ. It is a Book and a message Satan hates, and a Book demons detest and fear and will blaspheme in any deliverance or exorcism done, a phenomenon I have personally witnessed dozens of times. It is one of the completely unchanging variant during every deliverance I have ever been involved in. If Satan and his demons hate God's Word so much, we need to understand how much power God has invested in that Word, so much that He has placed His Word above His Name. (Psalm 138:2) It is the only weapon that is *sure* to challenge the lies of the coming New World Order and religious whore of Babylon – a religious system that will drink the blood of the saints and trample the pages of the Holy Scriptures of God and treat them with contempt and casualness, with the unattached demeanor of a child that tears out pages of a book he does not like anymore.

May God deliver the remnant of true believers from such a spiritually devastating outcome, and once again, establish His people in *truth* - the truth of the Word of God. "If the foundations be destroyed, what can the righteous do?" (Psalm 11:3)

Chapter Fourteen

The Discernment Gene and the Nature of Lies

One of the things that have greatly concerned me in the last couple of decades concerning the matters I am writing of here is the almost utter lack of discernment in the church as well as the almost utter lack of *concern* over these issues. The haze of deception has slowly pulled its misty veil over the eyes of believers, leaders and watchmen alike until trying to talk to someone about them often becomes a frustrating exercise in futility.

I remember spending a great deal of time on Hollywood Boulevard during my early Christian days, passing out Christian literature and telling people about Jesus. In some ways, we must have looked just like the *other* five hundred groups that were out there passing out religious stuff! There was everyone from the Hare Krishna people to the Tony Alamo cult, to Satanists, witches, Urantia cult, and even the "First Church of Spiritual Sexuality" that had their own "temple" staffed by very spiritual prostitutes.

It was a spiritual microcosm of the big world. It has always been like this: a spiritual world filled with thousands of demons and thousands of spiritual lies and deceptions, and occasionally, truth-tellers sent to reach those caught in the lies. It was like that with Paul. He was constantly going into Pagan cities and having nose to nose confrontations with sorcerers, religious deceivers, and demonized followers. He would have been right at home on Hollywood Boulevard.

Part of the problem with spiritual lies is that they sound good and reasonable - to a point. That is the lure. They have an appeal to our unredeemed, fleshly nature. They can appeal to our carnal mind. I remember being a year old baby Christian, recently redeemed from the world of occult lies but still working out the mental damage the occult brought. I was walking down Hollywood Boulevard and two very nice and persuasive people grabbed me and started fast-talking me about my life. They were very accurate; I was hurting. I didn't feel loved. My family was a mess. They managed to persuade me to come inside their building and take a "test." They had me put my hands around two cylinder type things with wires attached to them and an "E-meter" device with a needle in the middle that moved according to how I answered their questions. They asked, I answered. They shook their heads and finally concluded that I was a total mess and that they could help me get "cleared" of all the psychological baggage if I joined them. In the interest of literary truthfulness, I may not have exact recall of my next words, but I *did* laugh and say something to the effect that they had me put my hands around tin cans attached to a two dollar meter and supposedly could tell I was a psychological mess, and *who* was the crazy one? No, thank you...

I had just avoided being recruited and trapped for a lifetime in the highly persuasive and spiritually destructive cult of Scientology. Some of it sounded so good, so right, especially to those who have not been previously bitten by Lucifer's persuasive lies. Thank God I had already been. It was like an inoculation with venom that, when Jesus cured me, was an instant aversion to all things occultic, in whatever deceptive form it came in.

One evening we were passing out literature and a man started dialoging with me about his religion. To this day I cannot remember if he was a Krishnan or a Mormon or a Wiccan or any of the others. I just knew that as I stood trying to share the Gospel of Jesus with him, he just nodded and smiled serenely as if he were talking to a pathetic little child who did not understand. The more I talked, the more he smiled, his eyes shining with a demonic glitter that I was very familiar with. Finally I just spoke raw truth to him. "You are deceived. You are a slave of Satan, and unless you surrender your life to Jesus and repent of your sins, you are going to be spiritually damned forever." I said it calmly but I said it in words that demons clearly understood, so I was not surprised when the glittery eyes were suddenly replaced with a blackness and an evil and a hatred so raw I literally jumped back a step, as this formerly nice and understanding person let out a stream of vile cursing and violent threatening that completely unmasked the enemy's face and put this conversation in real context, as it always should be. It wasn't about sharing opinions over a nice cup of tea. It was about truth versus the lie.

So much for "dialoguing." So much for "having a conversation about God."

These two incidents were my first lessons in the nature of lies and how we handle them. First, the lie can be sweet, persuasive, and seductive, and seem logical and right. Second, when you stop playing the devil's game of "dialoguing" and verbal sparring and speak the plain language of truth, the mask will come off and the real powers behind the lies the person has accepted will be exposed. Those under the control of those lies may suddenly become angry and undone – the complete opposite of their formerly calm exterior. The rage of demonic forces surfaces because they have been forced into the light.

Paul found himself followed by a woman who I think any evangelist would be proud to have as a P.R. Person. She followed Paul and Silas and his crew and began crying out, "These men are the servants of the most high God, who show to us the way of salvation!" (Acts 16:17) She apparently did this for several days until Paul, "greatly annoyed" turned around and spoke, not to the girl, but to the *spirit of divination* that was in her, that was speaking through her, to come out of her. And it did.

If it were today, we would have no doubt commended her for her zeal, perhaps taken her aside and asked if she wanted to be on our leadership team. I am not joking. There is that little discernment left in the church.

This story not only underlines the true nature of spiritual warfare – that it is beyond words and not about words — but also illustrates an extremely important point about deception. The devil is in the details.

I have been told that when you get to the Greek root words of this passage, she was actually saying, "Listen to them. They show you *a* way to salvation." Just a tiny little detail…right? Wrong. It was the killing detail. Demons only speak half truth and twisted truth. They couldn't say they were showing *the* way. It was *a* way, as in, all paths lead to God, but here's *a* path you need to listen to. The end game here was to distract from the message being proclaimed and also to twist the message. I don't know how many times I have preached over the years when someone suddenly walks in out of nowhere or gets up and starts quoting scripture right in the middle of my message. They are not speaking by the Spirit but driven by a *demonic* spirit that cannot stand the truth to be proclaimed and will actually use the Bible to silence truth. Surprised? You shouldn't be. The devil knows the Bible better than most preachers, and he knows how to use it. (Read Matthew 4 for a full account of Satan's expertise as a Bible scholar).

The nature of lies is that it is rarely a big lie that snags the unprepared. It is little ones, sweet ones, almost right ones. As I said, the devil is in the details. A good example of that to me is when I was visiting friends for a few days. They had been given a book to read and asked what I thought of it. I recognized the author as an Emergent writer, so I must have looked rather obvious as I shrugged my shoulders and told them I hadn't read it. Knowing me as he does, my friend asked me to stay up that night so he could read portions of the book and ask what I thought was wrong with it. My problem was that nearly everything was wrong with it, but if you are not skilled to look beyond the surface and discern, you can miss it completely.

A side note: One thing that absolutely confounds me is the total non-reaction of believers to these things. When I first watched the Rob Bell "Bullhorn" DVD, my skin was crawling. It was a visceral, Holy Spirit reaction to the wrongness of Bell and his New Age teachings, even before I understood the full extent of it. When I first read Brian McLaren's *The Secret Message of Jesus*, I was so stirred and angry at this Christless, Crossless, Jesus-less mess he was presenting as Jesus' "hidden message" that I could hardly underline the offending passages *fast* enough, and through it all I just kept repeating to myself, "How come nobody *gets* this?" That was in the beginning of this new and first wave of the coming FutureChurch tsunami when the books and DVD's of this nature were a bit of an aberration. Now we are in the full swell of the wave and Christian bookstores are absolutely glutted with this material. Few are even raising a voice against it, outside of a few brave ministries that are discounted and ridiculed as "bloggers" by the Purpose-Driven and Emergent attack squads.

My friend, who was in some ways gratefully out of the loop of all of this on either side, simply read portions of this Emergent book and asked me what I thought was the problem with it. The first passage was about the author setting up a "confessional" booth on an atheistic campus, and when people came out of curiosity, the author would proceed to confess all the horrible sins of the church to unbelievers and apologize for the church being so horrible.

"What's wrong with that?" my friend asked. I told him I was not responsible for the crusades. A corrupt church was, but I was not there, and I was not them. In fact, I found a letter in Charisma magazine recently very insightful in this regard. The writer, a Native American, wrote:

"We hear a lot of empty rhetoric from some co-called Native American leaders telling non-Native people and the church in America how they need to apologize for past atrocities. But we Native Christians are not sitting here on the reservation waiting for an apology from the white man or anyone else. We have a lot of real-world issues just like you. We don't need any more apologies. Things are so bad here on the reservation; and only one thing will change things for us Native people: God. Don't bring us religious Christianity. Bring us the God of the Bible."

We would do well to heed this advice, and stop making misdirected apologies for crimes we did not commit, and go about bringing the Gospel that has the power not only to heal past wounds but to change broken lives into life-changing examples of the power and grace of God in Jesus Christ.

Jesus didn't tell us to go into all the world and say we're sorry for the terrible things Christians do. And while an unbeliever may be impressed with your "differentness" from the Jonesboro Baptist Church that is filled with hatred and unchristian behavior, it still will not bring them to salvation through Jesus. Because the message is not, "We're sorry we're so bad. Will you love us now? Can we persuade you to talk to us a little about Jesus? He's so misunderstood..." No. The message is, "It's not about you not believing because of bad people calling themselves "Christians," there are plenty of them obviously. The issue is, if you are completely separated from God because of your own sins and selfishness and if you don't turn around, give your life to Jesus and accept His blood sacrifice for forgiveness, you are not saved and will spend eternity separated from God." Bad Christian behavior is never allowed by God as an excuse to reject salvation through Jesus.

Before my friend went on, I told him that he was going to eventually learn that the writer was anti-Bush, anti-fundamentalist with a strictly social gospel message who stereotypes believers who do not fit the new Emergent model. "How do you know?" my friend said. "Trust me and read on," I told him. Within a few pages, the author said something to the effect of, "I have a problem with my Bush-loving, crazy fundamentalist Republican friends who do not take seriously Jesus' command to feed the poor." "Stop there," I said. "What's wrong with that statement?" My friend stopped and thought about it carefully, and a light went on. "Jesus didn't command us to feed the poor, right?" He got it.

Should we feed the poor? Absolutely. The Apostles made it a priority. But did Jesus *command* us to? No, He did not. He told us we would always have the poor with us. But He did not *command* us to feed them. Why is that important? Because the minute we start changing the Word of God, even a little bit, then it's open to all kinds of omissions and additions. If once you begin to proclaim it to say what it does not, you are pulling at a thread that will start to unravel the whole fabric of truth. Almost without exception, every cult was started by its leader taking a scripture out of context or changing what the scripture said, or finding verses that supported his or her particular view, and built a doctrine on it. That is why it *is* important when someone implies that the Bible says something that it does not.

Unfortunately, this goes right over the heads of a lot of Christians who spend little or no time actually reading the Bible. But even more well-read Christians can miss it. For example, after presenting some of this information at a meeting, one man pointed out that Jesus *did* command us to feed the poor because He said, "I was hungry and you did not feed me." I pointed out that it still was not a *command*. It was an *observation*. Yes, Jesus took the matter of taking care of the poor very seriously, and so should we. But that does not give us the right to play fast and loose with the Word of God to get it to say or imply something that it does not. Again, the devil is in the details, and once you begin to pull on just one thread of truth, the whole thing will eventually unravel.

I have never been more concerned than I am now that the "discernment gene" has been programmed right out of the church. I am appalled at the many televangelists who have given false prophecies, who harangue people for money, or who are teaching things that are so flimsy doctrinally that they would not withstand even a simple debate — and yet Christians excuse them and justify their errors and continue to support them. Are we so terrified of offending people or saying anything negative about a "man or woman of God" that we will let the truth take a backseat and be put in second place?

I know it is not easy to speak truth, especially when the people involved are so nice and so sincere. But that is how we have gotten to be so void of discernment. When we fail to raise the bar and keep out the wolves of false teachings, false prophecies and false teachers, we have then opened the floodgate to any illusion or lie that comes along.

A number of years ago I had one of my most painful lessons on the subtlety of deception and how difficult, yet necessary, it was for me to address this deception. I had read a book by a very well known woman whose brother was one of the most powerful men in the world. She was a Christian, raised Baptist and strong in the Word of God. She had written a powerful and profound book on emotional healing that I found both helpful to myself and to those I was ministering to. I wrote to her and she responded. We began a long and warm correspondence that developed into a true spiritual kinship and affection.

I was extremely honored when she invited me to her ranch retreat for a weekend workshop. I arrived late Friday afternoon, greeted her and settled in. She seemed very glad to see me, and we talked for quite a while before I took my leave to wait for the evening session.

There were famous people from around the world at this event — all of them hurting and looking for healing. I felt blessed to be there.

All was well until the evening session. The song leader began to lead the crowd of fifty or sixty people in some well-known Christian choruses. During the next song he asked us to grab the shoulders of the person in front of us and massage them as we sang. I felt suddenly very queasy. I dismissed this early warning alarm of the Holy Spirit, thinking it was just because I do not like to be touched by strangers. But I went along with it.

Then my friend got up and introduced a man she spoke of as her mentor and spiritual father. He would be leading the weekend's workshops.

The minute this gentleman began to speak, I felt like I was going to be ill. My stomach began to churn even before he opened his mouth. Then he said, among other things, that we were going to talk about God, whoever we conceived him or her to be. (Second warning bell.) He spoke about God in you, Christ in you, and the Bible, which contains the words of God. (By this time, I had a full panel of warning lights on, because nearly everything he said was straight out of the New Age dictionary).

We dismissed and waited for supper. I made several attempts to speak to my friend. It must have been obvious to her that I was alarmed, because she kept dodging me. She kept putting other people in front of her to make sure I could not reach her. Now I was really alarmed.

The next day I went to the men's session taught by her "mentor and spiritual father." Within the first ten minutes he told this group of twenty or twenty-five men that "Jesus cussed just like a real man would," and that Jesus had married Mary Magdalene and had children. I couldn't restrain myself any longer. I stood up, pointed at him, and said, "You, sir, are a liar and a false teacher, and I am *not* going to

162

sit here and let you deceive these men!" The spell was broken — just like with the Hare Krishna man I wrote of in the beginning of this chapter. All hell broke loose. The men were angry, confused, some even crying. The gentleman finally dismissed the class when he saw that the chaos had effectively ended his teaching session.

I went outside and stood by the fence. He finally came over and said, "Son, I used to be like you. I used to believe the Bible was the Word of God. But I grew up and you will too." I said, "Sir, I would rather die than even come to be like you or believe what you do now."

I left without being able to speak at all to my friend. I wrote her a letter expressing my love and concern when I got home. Rather than answer it herself, she allowed another one of her New Age "mentors" from another state to write me, calling me an ignorant fundamentalist who had no right to say anything at all.

She eventually lost her health and her life. I did eventually write a letter expressing again my concern and love and telling her that I only cared about her walk with God and meant her no injury. She wrote a conciliatory letter to me just before she died. It broke my heart. I was sad that a godly woman had been seduced by men of deception and there seemed to be no one around her that had the discernment — or the guts — to act on that discernment.

The nature of lies is that they will elude exposure at any cost. Once they have a foothold, exposing them will be painful and costly, and it will often cost precious friendships. But we cannot afford not to. Jesus said, "If therefore the light that is in thee be darkness, how great is that darkness!" (Matthew 6:23) There is a darkness that disguises itself as light. Discernment is the only weapon that can search it out and bring it to the true light. May God raise up a new generation with discernment as clear as day and as sharp as a razor, sending them into the midst of the darkness of the FutureChurch to shatter that darkness with the shining light of truth.

Chapter Fifteen

All On The Same Page

—∿—

I was at Bible School in Oakland California as a young 18 year old wanting to serve Jesus. It was a wonderful school in many ways, and to this day I have nothing but warm memories of the pastors and teachers there.

One of their worship songs, though, really disturbed me, to the point that after a few times I couldn't even sing it. It went like this:

As the river flows, flows into the sea, and loses its identity,
That's how it is with you and me in God

I am sure it was unintentional, but this song smacked of all the occult teaching God had delivered me from. Let go of yourself, your ego, give yourself over to the Divine Mind, etc. etc. I had given myself up and over so much that all that was left was a shell. I did not like this song. I was *not* going to lose my identity in some spiritual river and blend into one big stream with everyone else. Been there, done that. That was *not* how it was with you and me in God. If anything, God taught me the *value* of who I was individually. Jesus died for *me*. Jesus came to *me*. Jesus redeemed *me*. Paul said we were one body, but many members. For the first time, I felt like a real person, a whole person. Now I was being told that I had to become a blob, identity-less for Jesus. No thank you.

I am intensely bothered by the uniformity and conformity I see taking form in the evangelical West. I am probably alone in my feeling that denominations are a *good* thing. If we were all in the same building, we would no doubt strangle each other. Denominations allow us – if we handle those differences in a godly way – to remain true to Biblical absolutes and give room for practical preferences. Denominational differences have been the cause of horrible suffering and rancor at times – but all in all, they allow us to go where we feel we can serve God with the most liberty.

The Bible does speak a great deal about unity. Paul spoke of us all coming to unity in the faith. Jesus prayed, "That they may be one, even as You and I are one." (John 17:22) There is no question that unity of heart and mind is something that has been greatly lacking in the church yet is greatly valued by God.

However, this unity can never be at the cost of sacrificing Biblical absolutes. These things make us who we are: Faith in Jesus as the only Son of God, who died on a cross for our redemption, who rose from the dead and is coming again to judge the living and the dead, the absolute sovereignty of the Word of God, the scriptures, the virgin birth of Jesus; these are what define historical Christianity, if you will. For every step we make to lessen, loosen and liberalize those things, we take a step closer to New Age religion and the coming New World Luciferian Order. Paul spoke of the scriptures and the teachings of Jesus and of Peter and the other Apostles as things that *must* be passed down to others, and he said if anyone was contrary minded, he was confident God would show them. (Philippians 3:15) He acknowledged that there would be differences; that is why he said, "If it be possible, as much as lieth in you, live peaceably with all men." (Romans 12:18) But no matter the differences, there was a uniformity of basic teaching that has sustained the real church for over 2,000 years, despite the multitudinous efforts to discard the scriptures and build the church on feelings and conjecture and humanistic social causes. God has always had the steady light of truth burning — and He always will.

My concern today is that there is a push toward a kind of uniformity and conformity in the name of unity that has nothing to do with Jesus' desire that we may be one. For it is not a unity that is built on prayer, humility, and working together for the sake of the Gospel. It is a unity that is based around a new template for "doing church." I am afraid the Purpose-Driven template is a very good example of what I mean. Purpose-Driven unity is a silencing of anyone who doesn't "get with the program." They call them Lone Rangers.

In the Purpose-Driven program, the emphasis on scripture study is rather minimal. Care groups tend to be more topical and psychological. Actual Bible Study is not a huge component of the program, and scripture references, though used, are usually relegated to a few power point slides from some flimsy "Bible" like *The Message*. Messages tend to be about coping, problems, jobs, family, romance, etc. In other words, our human needs become the center of the message. I do not see that as a Biblical template. The Bible and the Gospel of Jesus are to be the center of the message and we are to bring the scriptures to bear on our problems for solutions. You don't apply a nail to the end of a hammer to drive it in. You apply the hammer to the nail. The hammer is the Word. Our problems are the nail. Otherwise, we are just a self-help club.

The Purpose-Driven model is based on the idea that we all need to "be on the same page." This in itself is a New Age concept and it is a corporate model that we adopted as the church. It means, practically, that everyone should be teaching and believing the exact same thing all the time. This is "being on the same page." It has a limited value. Unfortunately, it usually makes what the Purpose-Driven leader feels is most important for people to hear preeminent, not the Word of God. Everyone is expected to fall in line. This bothers me — not because I'm not a "team player," to use another New Age buzzword, but because it teaches people not to study, nor to dig into the Word of God for themselves, but to just go along to get along. It makes for warm discussions and shallow growth levels. It makes people feel good to discuss problems, read a verse and go home. You don't even have to question anything or see what the scriptures say for yourself. It's pretty much thought out for you. That's great if your pastor is actually teaching solid stuff. But with more and more blending of Emergent "conversations" with Purpose-Driven programs, Bible studies are becoming a thing of the past and coffee klatch spirituality prevails. When care groups become discussions about the spiritual content of "I Love Lucy," we are in serious trouble indeed. There is no hardcore prayer, no solid teaching and no real growth. Just nice, harmless stuff that makes sure we're all "on the same page." "As the river flows, flows into the sea, and loses its identity, that's how it is with you and me in God."

The New Age very much wants us all to be on the same page. That way, we can slowly be brought into their book under the chapter, "Harmless Christians, easily led."

Martin Luther was part of the groupthink in his day until he actually read the scriptures and realized that salvation came by faith in Jesus Christ, not by works and mortification. He hammered a list of theses to the Wittenburg door, and the rest is history. He thought for himself, read for himself and allowed the Holy Spirit to teach him. These days, that is almost considered heresy. It makes you a "Lone Ranger." You are no longer a "team player." You are not part of the Groupthink.

I loved Bible School because we had long and heated debates into the night about any number of issues: Can you lose your salvation? When is Jesus returning? Can a Christian have a demon? And then we ended while rarely really agreeing, yet hugging each others' neck and saying "God bless you anyway!" That was true "unity in diversity."

The *new* model of Christianity is a slow elimination of all the scriptural things that divide us, through the method of destroying the foundations of the things we are standing upon, making the Word of God a weak bunch of stories or just verses to help us live better and happier, and marginalizing, ridiculing and outcasting those who actually believe that the truth of the Word of God is unquestionable, and worth fighting for.

I am not on the same page with these things. I am not a team player with the architects of the coming FutureChurch. I am, very much, a Lone Ranger with a Bible in my hand and a few companions along the way who will not compromise truth for the sake of false unity which is really corporate organization, New Age socialization, and crowd control in the name of "the Kingdom come."

Hi ho, Silver, and away.

Chapter Sixteen

Signs and Wonders

—⟋ℳ⟍—

The Purpose-Driven, Seeker-Friendly and Emergent movements are removing the true power of God from the church. They are replacing it with a new social apparatus for fellowship. The Emergent Church is replacing the raw Gospel of sin, salvation, death and resurrection with doubt, blurred identity and a weakened or nonexistent confidence in the Word of God – a kind of care-bear Christianity that harms – and heals – no one. They are readjusting and refitting the New Gen believers to be a harmless but useful social group that will fit in seamlessly with the coming One World Religion. But there is one area in the church that has remained relatively intact and unperverted by New Age thought – until now. I am referring to the intercessory prayer, prophetic, and signs and wonders movement in the church.

If you have already decided that all of that is of the devil and that Charismatics and Pentecostals are all deluded and deceived, I do not share that opinion at all. I believe in the power of the Holy Spirit. I was spiritually raised almost entirely in Charismatic and Pentecostal circles. I attended a Spirit-filled Bible school. Although my theology is more Baptist in many ways than Pentecostal, no one believes in and longs for the true power of God to be at work more than this writer. So if I've lost you, I'm sorry. I can't write this chapter as an anti-Charismatic because I am not. I write as one of them because I have spent most of my life among them and because I have a deep and crucial investment in this movement. I believe only an insider can speak to it and have a chance of being heard. So to those who are part of these movements, please hear me. I have seen healings that were medically impossible. My life was saved at least once by a physically present and manifest angel. I have done battle with the demonic and participated in deliverances for many years. God has twice spoken audibly – literally – to me. I have dreamed dreams and seen visions. No one can ever convince me that God's Holy Spirit is not going to pour out His Spirit on all flesh in these last days.

With all of my heart I fear being one who would ever "limit the Holy One of Israel."

But I cannot warn of the FutureChurch deception without including some serious concerns and warnings to the intercessory, prophetic and signs and wonders movement.

Not all that glitters is Gospel.

With all the good and legitimate Holy Spirit work that came with the Pentecostal and Charismatic rush of the 1970's, a lot of junk crept in also. And I'm going to name it as I see - and saw it - because I was there.

At age fifteen, I was occult riddled, hateful, a heavy drinker and nearly a pack a day smoker. Then I was powerfully saved. But I had been coughing up blood and I was terrified.

A faith preacher came to the house meeting where I had gotten saved. He prayed for me, and God healed me instantly - 100%.

When he shot like a rocket to the top of the "health, wealth, and prosperity" movement, I cringed. That movement had become powerful, but was full of scriptural errors and excesses.

I do believe God blesses His people – sometimes extraordinarily, sometimes financially. He has promised, according to Philippians 4:19, to supply all of our needs (not greeds) according to His riches in glory by Christ Jesus. But Paul clearly gave the template when he said, "Not that I speak in respect to want; for I have learned, in whatsoever state I am, therewith to be content. I know both how to be abased, and I know how to abound: everywhere and in all things I am instructed both to be full and to be hungry, both to abound and to suffer need. I can do all things through Christ which strengtheneth me." (Philippians. 4:11-13)

But in a short period of time, an entire movement based on a few out of context scriptures become the basis for a nationwide teaching that convinced Christians that God wanted them to be rich, healthy and prosperous.

One of the primary principles for nearly every off-balanced movement or teaching in the church is that they focus on a few specific passages to the ignoring – or explaining away – of others. A wise person once said that the truth never lies in just "It is written," but in "It is written," and "again, it is written." In other words, the truth is in the balance of *all* scripture concerning a subject. That is why Paul's passage is so vital; he knew poverty and prosperity, illness and health, weakness and strength, and he learned to be content in them *all*, because He accepted Jesus' Lordship over his life and all his circumstances. He also knew the difference between what was Holy Spirit allowed and what was satanically sent.

The Prosperity Gospel, as it has been called, has many good people and some good thoughts. But this movement have not done justice to the Word of God. They have taken Psalms 1:3 concerning the godly which reads, "whatsoever he doeth shall prosper" and have taken that to mean the godly person will be rich. But the Hebrew word for "prosper" simply means "push forward," not "get rich." The prosperity preachers also took 3 John 2, which says, "Beloved I wish above all things that you may prosper and be in health even as your soul prospers," and used it as a proof text that God wants you to be rich. But a small amount of research uncovers that the greeting, "May you prosper and be in health" was a common letter greeting in that day, much like "Have a nice day" or "God bless you." John just added a spiritual dimension to a common greeting – that's all.

Hebrews 11, called the "faith chapter," is an awesome portion of scripture. The matter of faith is very important. But the last part of that chapter speaks of those who were sawn in half, lived in caves, were martyred, persecuted, etc. – of whom, the writer said, the world is not worthy. It is a passage I saw completely ignored by the growing faith and prosperity movement. I saw many innocent people get hurt because of this teaching that God wanted them rich and that illness was always a product of a lack of faith. The Prosperity Gospel was gaining ground at the same time that several other very questionable movements with really bad fruit and weak scriptural foundations were gaining ground: The Shepherding movement, the Kingdom Now movement, and unbalanced deliverance-type ministries.

Five years after this famous prosperity preacher prayed over me (and I thank God he did, and thank Jesus for the healing He did) I was attending Bible School. Halfway through the first year, this man who had prayed for me for healing came to speak.

He told the students that if they were cleaning houses to pay for their tuition, they were out of God's will because God wanted them to be prosperous, not to do menial work. I just cringed. Jesus Himself took a towel and washed the feet of His disciples. This man's teaching had gone from slightly off to really unscriptural. (Error is a progressive disease). He was teaching serious error, and no one was calling him on it. It broke my heart, as he was the one God had used to heal me of my affliction.

This was during the Watergate cover-up. I was absolutely appalled when this man "prophesied" in an article in the school magazine, "Thus says the Lord, my servant Richard Nixon is innocent, and I will vindicate him, saith the Lord." Well, you know how that turned out. And yet, he went to the top of the Prosperity Movement, where he remains today, despite him having given a *blatant false prophecy.*

Even more disturbing, five years later this man came to our city and held a huge crusade at the civic center. The transformation in him was stunning and the presence in that place was electric. But it was not the Holy Spirit; it was something else. He taught that we are the body of Christ....and since we are, then he is the body of Christ...therefore, he is...Christ. He was preaching a page straight out of New Age theology. Here was a once godly man who, through little changes and re-interpreting of the scriptures, became someone who was proclaiming himself to be Christ. It was a stunning example to me of progressive deception within the church. Even more disturbing was that everyone was treating his errors as if they were just little faux pas. Why were these things not challenged? Confronted?

One of the things I frequently hear when someone goes into error is, "But they teach a lot of good things too!" And yet a little leaven leavens the whole loaf. "Don't throw out the baby with the bathwater!" But spiritual lies are not bathwater nor is the church a baby. They are snakes in the stream of the Body of Christ. Jesus said, "Either make the tree good, and his fruit good; or else make the tree corrupt, and his fruit corrupt: for the tree is known by his fruit." (Matthew 12:33) We have gotten so forgiving and so liberal in allowing errors, false prophecies, false words, and bad doctrine that the signs and wonders and prophetic end of the church is *already in the midst* of becoming a mixed stream of half-truth and half-lies, and, unless there is great awakening and repentance in its leadership and followers, it will eventually end up in complete deception. Allowing a lie means that the truth will always be over-come and buried by that lie as the leaven overcomes the loaf. It's just the way it works.

Unfortunately, for all the good and genuine in the world of the gifts of the Holy Spirit that I still believe in, people tend to elevate teachers, prophets, bishops, and apostles and give them an almost godlike status. They soon become unapproachable. If someone questions them, someone will say, "Touch not mine anointed!" There was even teaching for a while about death coming to those who talked negatively about "God's anointed." I understand Biblical authority and anointing. But even Paul "withstood Peter to the face, for he was to be blamed." (Galatians 2:11) I understand there is a Biblical way to do these things, such as not to accuse an elder except before two or three witnesses. (1Timothy 5:19) But the problem is, when one brings up certain issues, people say, "Well, have you tried to talk to them about it? Have you gone to them?" These people are fairly unclear as to how it works today. You can't *reach* them. They have bodyguards. They have screeners. They have people that make sure criticism and correction never reaches them at all. If I could, I would, but the current state of mega-fame in evangelical America makes that quite impossible.

I am concerned when certain people, who are called prophets by both the Christian media and their own press releases, have pronounced disaster on certain dates and the dates pass with no disaster. There is neither retraction nor repentance. Sometimes they explain it away: "God changed his mind because people prayed."

That is a very dangerous game. In the Old Testament you were stoned to death if you gave a false prophecy. But with many of today's "prophets," no one has any ability to call them into account and the flock is fleeced without even a "baaaa" of protest.

I am concerned that so many of these major teachers, self-proclaimed prophets, bishops, and apostles are allowed to set themselves up, take truckloads of money in the name of ministry and no one can stop them. One couple just divorces, divides up their ministry and goes on as if nothing happened. One Bishop beats his wife publicly not long after their million dollar wedding. One high level popular teacher won't even come to speak for less than $250,000 a night plus first class everything. They have gatherings, honor themselves, command their people to follow and obey them and believe their words, while offering after offering is given to them and people continue to buy books and DVD's to keep up with the latest "revelation" or find out who has been "anointed" for what office. I am not being facetious. This is really happening. I am really convinced that if Jesus were here, He would overturn these moneychangers and self-appointed leaders so fast it would be breathtaking. But as it is, people are so hungry for an encounter with God, that they have been willing to accept any word, any teaching, and any proclamation from these people, simply because they say it is so, and they say it with great command and charisma.

I believe completely in the gifts of the Spirit that Paul listed in which the Apostles and early believers walked in. I have experienced and walked in these things my whole adult life. But because of the absolutely exotic and unscriptural nature of the new wave of teaching that is coming through many parts of this movement, my concern – no, my spirit's wrenching cry – is that a hole as wide as eternity is being opened up to false miracles and lying signs and wonders, yet few are discerning it, confronting it, or dealing with it. Just as I fear that the Purpose-Driven, Seeker-Friendly and Emergent Church movements are removing the true power of God from the church through programs, prosperity preaching and corporate kingdom building as well as removing faith in the Word of God and the urgency of the Coming of Jesus and the end times, so, too, I fear that lying signs and wonders are coming into the back door of the church in order to deceive those who are hungry for the true supernatural power of God, and yet who have no discernment and no willingness to discern. It is providing them with a mind-blowing supernatural counterfeit that will open them up to the demonic realm like nothing else. It is creating a vast following of signs and wonders addicts that go from conference to conference just to get a fix and a spiritual high. It is accustoming them to the "wonders" and "miracles" that the false prophet and antichrist will have even more abundantly, and leave people wondering if this indeed may be Jesus who has returned. Do you understand my concern?

You can find reams of information on the internet that questions Benny Hinn, TBN, and a number of others in the signs and wonders movement. I am very careful how I approach this chapter knowing that I may be perceived by them as just one more "heresy hunter". But I am writing as one of them. I write this to the heart of them. I have a *right* and a responsibility to do so, not as an outside critic, but as someone who is still on the inside, still longing to see a genuine outpouring of the Holy Spirit in this last hour. Please hear me. More is at stake than you know.

You cannot read the scriptures without understanding that the false prophet and the antichrist are going to absolutely astound people with the supernatural and "miraculous." (1 Thessalonians 2:9)

I believe one of the walls Satan *must* tear down in the church for the FutureChurch to come together is in the area of the supernatural. He is doing it through "Christian Yoga," "breath prayers," Hindu-like breath-praying exercises, "imagining," "vision casting," "visualizing," and so on. "Experiencing God" or "experiencing the divine" is already taking precedent over the Word of God. Experience has become Lord - not Jesus. But the scriptures command us to "test the spirits" - test every experience, every voice, every dream, vision or revelation.

Without exception, the most powerful New Age teachers had an "experience," usually accompanied by a vision, dream or voice that claimed to be "God," "Jesus," "Ascended Masters," or angels, and caused them to turn from Biblical truth to exotic, attractive demonic lies. The experiences overruled all common sense, reason, and objective truth.

Recently I was listening to New Age teacher Eckhart Tolle, author of *A New Earth* and *The Power of Now* in his series of on-line teachings with Oprah Winfrey, who has turned him into the newest mega-seller and star. I was astounded that so much excitement was generated over Tolle and his message. The message was little more than a rehash of the same New Age "revelations" from the 1980's and before. Tolle spoke senseless, but impressive sounding, "truths" as Oprah reverently wowed over his proclamations such as "Be in the moment," or "As you walk up the stairs, be in every moment of walking up the stairs," Tolle and others, such as Marianne Williamson and Esther Hicks are like the New Age version of "regifting." Satan rewraps New Age ideas from previous years, and no one will know it's the same old thing. In their world, *experience* is all – not God's truth.

The mesmerizing quality of Tolle and the mesmerized responses from the callers reminded me that the great deception to come will be built as much on supernatural seduction and mesmerization as it will be on twisted truth. It will be an abandonment and suspension of spiritual reason and scriptural truth while being overtaken by the force of *experience*. People say, "I had a real supernatural experience and it changed me! Doesn't that prove it is from God?" No, it does not. Unfortunately, since Satan is hardly even mentioned in the FutureChurch teaching formats, many believers have not been taught that Satan comes as an angel of light and is capable of imitating and counterfeiting supernatural events and "miracles," just like the manifestations of the magicians of Pharaoh. The scriptures make it plain that false supernatural manifestations will be an earmark of the last days. But because the FutureChurch is being taught to ignore the devil and people are being told to ignore what one Christian writer referred to as "New Age silliness," the church no longer understands that Satan is quite capable of imitating all the gifts of the Holy Spirit such as tongues, healing, prophecy, and words of knowledge. If we have any hope of avoiding falling for the false supernatural, we need to be trained in truth and know how to "test the spirits." (1 John 4:1)

I am told that bank tellers in training at the major banks in New York start by just counting money for the first few weeks. They do nothing else. Then at some point a counterfeit bill is put in the stack. They detect it right away because they have been handling the real thing for so long that the fake one just stands out. That is how we are to be trained in truth. We must be so familiar with the real thing – the truth – the Word of God and so steeped and established in it, that not only will we detect false teaching, but if there is a counterfeit spiritual manifestation that takes place, everything in us will "feel the lie" because the true Word of God has become our absolute foundation of truth.

I have been to spiritualist meetings where many "supernatural gifts" were manifested. They looked just like the real thing. I have had demonized people show up at my evangelistic services and "preach the Word" right out of the Bible under demonic power and force. I knew these kinds of things could happen, because the Word of God warns us about "angels of light."

But in the mid 1980's I grew increasingly concerned that the false was really starting to take hold in the church. False prophecies were more frequent. Formerly sound Christian authors were suddenly teaching New Age tinged Christianity. One man wrote a book on why Jesus was coming back that year, which He did not, and the man followed it up with a book on how it was actually going to be the following year. Christians just kept buying his books anyway. A Christian pastor wrote a book on extensive visits he had from dog-petting angels, and after that, the books and teachings just got farther and farther off base. These books were flying off of the shelves. Christians couldn't get enough of these stories. Anyone who claimed a supernatural experience from the Spirit gained immediate credibility in the circles I was in. Few discerned, and if they did, they were dismissed as having a "critical spirit." I knew we were headed for serious trouble.

Fast forward to the 1990's. Suddenly I began hearing reports about the "laughter movement." At a local church, Christians were starting to bark like dogs, roar like lions and slither like snakes. Everything in me cried out against such manifestations. In the deepest occult groups, as well as Voodoo and Santeria groups, being taken over by an "animal spirit" is a common and sought-after experience. If you watched a video of a person being "ridden" by a Voodoo or

Santerian "god" and compared it to some of the videos of Christians being taken over and barking, growling, roaring, or slithering like a snake, the hair on the back of your head would stand up. They are virtually indistinguishable. Occult groups have animal totems and they call on those animal spirits to possess their supplicants (and sometimes victims) and suddenly, the people begin to act and sound just like that animal. These similar manifestations that Christians claimed were of the Holy Spirit were *not* from God. There is *zero* scriptural precedence for such a thing and scriptural precedence is *always* the first instrument of discerning and trying the spirits to see if they are from God.

I have seen people prayed for and "slain in the Spirit." I think there is a godly reality to this. When Solomon dedicated the temple, the Shekinah glory of God filled the temple so that the priests could not stand. (1 Kings 8:11) I confess that one time I was so over-whelmed by the Spirit of God during worship that I felt that I was "drunk in the Spirit" – completely overwhelmed by His love - so overcome that I had to be driven home. I have even had God fill me with so much joy that I just laughed out loud. There has been a genuine aspect to many of these unusual manifestations. But in time they have become something completely different.

When a "laughter crusade" came to my town I went just to see, to pray, to discern, maybe even (if I was wrong) to be touched by God.

I was shocked to see a large group of people running around the building, laughing, falling over, almost in a frenzy. The evangelist called local pastors who disagreed with him "cockroaches hiding under a rock." More unsettling, there was a man dressed in black with black sunglasses standing just a few feet behind the evange-list at all times like a bodyguard, or a CIA agent, or a 'handler" or something else.

In the background, there was an unmistakable sound of canned laughter that went off about every half minute during the evan-gelist's speech. It was an identical high pitched woman's voice, just quiet enough to almost be heard, but not without paying close attention. I cannot prove this, but it appears that they were using a subtle laugh track, perhaps to trigger laughing spells in case it didn't happen by itself.

By that time I was ready to go. I stood in the back of the auditorium as the evangelist had a CD and DVD "give away" and he sailed dozens of them across the auditorium as people, acting like trained seals, jumped up and down to try to get one, yelling, "Here, here, me! ME!" One CD broke a pastor's nose. I had to jump up and hit another one to the ground to keep a man from having a CD sink itself right between his eyes.

It was then that the conference coordinator came up and interrogated me. He had been watching me. He told me he was tired of critics and he could throw me out because he was the man in charge. Ironically, he boasted that he used to set up conferences for one of the most well-known and well-respected Evangelists in the country. I finally left. The display I saw at that meeting both from the evangelist, the attendees and the people in charge was truly upsetting and was definitely an artificially engineered imitation of spiritual manifestations. There was no sense of the Holy Spirit making this happen. It appeared to be just a contagious mass crowd reaction.

Conferences were beginning to get more and more out of control. The emotional pitch was becoming almost hysterical. People were screaming, jerking, slithering and making animal noises. One person even was making pig noises, which they jokingly called "The anoinking of the Spirit." I wish that were a joke, but it is not. To equate the Holy Spirit with an unclean animal is the height of demonic foolery and mockery. I am very cautious about these statements because the last thing I ever want to do is grieve the Holy Spirit, but I am speaking because that is exactly what these things are doing.

It seems to me that decades of unchecked, untested, and undiscerned "manifestations" has resulted in a broken wall in the one area in the church not quite touched by the New Age spirit, that of the miraculous. I had seen excesses all my life, but also the real, including Kathryn Kuhlman. But this was different. I sensed that something had broken into the Temple and brought in an unholy spirit that was not the Spirit of God, but "strange fire." (Leviticus 10:1)

In the midst of the first thoughts, prayers and preparations for the writing of this book, I received a very clear picture from God concerning the coming of lying signs and wonders to the church.

I saw a trickle, and then a literal flood enter into the back door of the church as the wall of discernment and truth crumbled. I knew that breaching this wall of protection and pouring false supernatural manifestations into the church was going to be a major component in preparing the FutureChurch to receive the antichrist spirit – and eventually the antichrist himself – and his "miracles" when he comes.

Within days of that revelation, someone brought me a set of CD messages from a local church. A visiting evangelist had preached for five nights. He was a former professor at the Bible school I attended. My friend was concerned enough to buy the set and have me listen to it.

I listened to five nights of excellent teaching. I found very little if anything that I disagreed with. My spirit resonated with much of what was said. But on the last CD, the evangelist made a statement that was terrifying. He said that as we got closer to the last days we would experience more and more of an "open heaven" and more miracles. He then said that we needed to be open to the possibility that we would start getting visitations from angels – and our departed loved ones. There it was: Necromancy in Christian disguise. There has been much talk about angels lately. But now they were taking Hebrews 12, which speaks of us being surrounded by a "great cloud of witnesses," and suggests that there are saints and loved ones that are breaking through to communicate with us. This evangelist unknowingly blew a psychic hole straight through the center of that church and its undiscerning members who believed every word of it. The Bible is so utterly clear about speaking to the dead – or them speaking to us – that Saul lost his life for trying it. Yet here was a well-known man of God slipping this in during the last part of a five night crusade.

Since then I have heard and seen all manner of manifestations. There are now ministries promoting Christian levitation -"transporting in the Spirit"- and more. The justification I have heard is, "Well, Satan is a counterfeiter, so there has to be a real for each counterfeit, and God is just showing Satan who the originator is!" That is the wrong answer. There is *not* a real for each counterfeit. There is not a real for necromancy. "Well, didn't Jesus speak to Moses and Elijah?" Yes. But Peter and the disciples did *not*. *Jesus* did, because Jesus is the Son of God He created them and knew them from the beginning.

However, the reverse is true – for every gift and miracle of God, Satan has a counterfeit – but it is a dangerous and misleading thing to think the opposite must be true. There are many occult practices that have *no* equal and real part in the Kingdom of God, such as Tarot card reading, palmistry, and crystal magick.

Next I heard about "gemstones" appearing out of nowhere. I had already heard about gold dust manifestations, and an "angel feathers" manifestation that actually turned out to be colored chicken feathers, but the gemstone manifestations were new to me. As with anything like this, I always approach such a thing with a heart that wants to know the truth and with a heart that is determined *not* to limit the Holy One of Israel or call something that is holy, unholy. But I also have to be willing to discern the truth, even if that offends my friends. That is how I approached this latest round of manifestations.

I had gone to a website that was posting videos and pictures of angels, oil manifestations, gold dust, and gemstones. I saw a video of an angel dancing around a fire. I honestly cannot say it was not an angel. It definitely was not just lights and shadows. It could have been a fallen angel, for all I know. But it was real.

I went to the gemstone photos and videos. They are authentic and have apparently been validated as flawless by certified gemologists. So to me, it was not a question as to whether they were real: the question was, were they from God? Remember that the devil is in the details. Just like the book whose author said Jesus commanded us to feed the poor when He did not, or the demonized girl who said about Paul and the disciples, "They show you *a* way to God," so a tiny detail in the "gemstone" story revealed the enemy's hand. In a video interview with people who had gemstones deposited on their property, a man said, "We were standing there and saw the angel, and she came up to us…"

Stop. There is no specific angel identified in scripture as female (although a case may be made for the two women who had wings like a stork in Zechariah 5:9, but they were not identified as angels and the Bible always identifies angels as such. And since storks are an unclean animal, it would at the least not be an angel from God.

Fallen ones, perhaps.) What is true is that even though you cannot find any scriptural evidence for a female angel, there *is* one group that is wildly fascinated with female angelology: The New Age followers. Female angels are very much part of their "theology," so to speak. Does this matter? I think it does, for it was the first clue that this manifestation may not be coming from the Kingdom of God, but from another kingdom where Satan can come as an angel of light.

I looked at other videos and they got stranger and stranger. One church had oil dripping down the walls and it had soaked through the pulpit Bible. They literally showed someone squeezing oil out of it. There was also gold dust and a big piece of carpet where a foot-print of huge dimensions was left in the carpet, which they had cut out as proof that an angel had visited.

By the time I finished all of this, with the attending proofs and statements that "we know these things are from God because they glorify God and Jesus," my head was swimming. These things were real and I did not – and could not – doubt the sincerity of the people it was happening to, or those who were promoting it. Elijah did some strange miracles too. I literally told the Lord, "Look, if this is from You, just drop a gem on my desk tonight, and I will preach this far and wide." And I meant it. But what came to me was, "Look up the miracles of Sai Baba." I was *not* expecting that answer.

Sathya Sai Baba is a guru from India who is known worldwide for the miraculous occurrences in his meetings. He has (or his familiar spirit has) supernaturally appeared in visions to people around the world who had *never heard of him*, telling them to come and follow him. He was a perfect example of signs and lying wonders in our present age.

Now, faced with all these new manifestations, I cautiously Googled Sai Baba and found a site that documented his "miracles."[1] (Caution: This is a highly occultic site, proceed with prayer if you wish to view these photos.) There I found dozens of photos of angelic type manifestations: gold powder, "sacred ash," gems and jewelry, you name it. These things were nearly identical to the manifesta-tions that were cropping up in prophetic circles.

You must judge for yourself what is of God and what is not. I am presenting this very cautiously because I truly believe there *is* a supernatural, miraculous that is Holy Spirit manifested, and I have seen it and I have walked in it and believe it with my whole heart. But these new manifestations seem to have no purpose at all. Miracles in the Bible had a *point.* People were healed, delivered, fed, saved, rebuked. But these new "miracles" seem to have little or no such fruit. They just excite people and cause people to seek after a sign and not Jesus Himself. "And when the people were gathered thick together, he began to say, This is an evil generation: they seek a sign; and there shall no sign be given it, but the sign of Jonas the prophet." (Luke 11:29) That is a very dangerous place for us to be, for the antichrist and false prophet *will* come with all signs and lying wonders. I am convinced that many FutureChurch believers will fall for it because they have never been taught to discern the false from the real. And it is getting harder to do.

One other disturbing thought. I had been reading the writings of some of those who are teachers in the "prophetic" movement. A number of them were obviously not from God, such as a lady who said that God showed her about "changing the molecular structure of atoms" and telling her He was going to heal the earth, which prompted her to proclaim that she would go to the rainforest and pray for the earth to be restored. (She would fit in perfectly in the Green New Age circles.)

But I came upon another article that was using scripture and explaining the root Hebrew words to make their point. I believe in doing that, except that the Hebrew words he chose were very familiar to me from the occult world. They were the Hebrew words that are used to describe the "sephirot"- or the "ten spheres" or "emanations" that lead to God that are part of the "Tree of Life," based on Hebrew magical teachings called the Kabbalah. Kabbalah is perhaps the purest – and most dangerous – occult working there is. It truly does have the capacity to kill if you get it wrong, make you insane, or to open the door into the angelic realm. And those that do have done so at their own peril. The one-third of the fallen angels who fell with Lucifer to earth have never ceased trying to pry those doors open from their world into ours in order to rule and reign here on earth, and over mankind. After I read this article it occurred to me, though I cannot prove it, that some of these Christians may in fact have been reading and practicing the Kabbalah (as they *have* been doing in many Messianic Jewish circles). They are perhaps justifying it by saying they are "redeeming it back to God." If they are doing this, then it is very possible that many of these "angelic visitations" and manifestations are indeed real – but they are *not* from God, but from the fallen ones. Let that sink in real good before you embrace without question the miraculous, just because it is miraculous.

One of the prime prophetic voices in this movement is carrying on a huge revival in Florida where all kinds of manifestations are taking place. According to former prophetic movement teacher Andrew Strom this man has apparently been teaching guided visualization. In the words of Strom, who is very alarmed about this man, "I myself have heard the tapes...of his 'third heaven visualization' teachings, and I want to tell you – they are straight out of the New Age handbook." Lynn Clark, a moderator for Strom's RevivalSchool.com website, shares her involvement with this man's teachings:

> **I decided to check (these teachers) out... and, ignorant of their 'third heaven' guided visualizations, attended... conferences and began to imagine third heaven visitations - guided visualization - still not realizing that these are actually spirits of darkness - the New Age calls them spirit guides - demons is what they are. And so I bought the teaching on third heaven visitations and brought it home to listen to.**
>
> **I was in my living room laying on the floor listening to the teaching on how to visualize the third heaven and what to say and was getting caught up into his teaching and all of a sudden I began to shake uncontrollably and jerk and groan, and no sooner had this taken place I became frozen stiff - I could not move any part of my body and I knew this was a demon trying to take hold of me, and so with all the effort I could muster I cried out, "God save me - Jesus help me" - and as soon as I cried out to the Lord my body went limp. God spared me that night and I will be forever grateful.**

I spent much of the night in tears asking God to forgive me - and renouncing all the hands laid on me and all the awful deception I had opened myself up to.[2]

The revival leader, Todd Bentley, has taught that he entered the third heaven and visited with Paul, who told him that he and Abraham wrote the book of Hebrews together, which is why it has no name. He says he has a female personal financial angel, Emma. Todd says this:

So when I need a financial breakthrough I don't just pray and ask God for my financial breakthrough. I go into intercession and become a partner with the angels by petitioning the Father for the angels that are assigned to getting me money: "Father, give me the angels in heaven right now that are assigned to get me money and wealth. And let those angels be released on my behalf. Let them go into the four corners of the earth and gather me money."

Todd continues:

EMMA, ANGEL Of The PROPHETIC

Now let me talk about an angelic experience with Emma. Twice Bob Jones asked me about this angel that was in Kansas City in 1980: "Todd, have you ever seen the angel by the name of Emma?" He asked me as if he expected that this angel was appearing to me. Surprised, I said, "Bob, who is Emma?" He told me that Emma was the angel that helped birth and start the whole prophetic movement in Kansas City in the 1980s. She was a mothering-type angel that helped nurture the prophetic as it broke out. Within a few weeks of Bob asking me about Emma, I was in a service in Beulah, North Dakota. "In the middle of the service I was in conversation with Ivan and another person when in walks Emma. As I

stared at the angel with open eyes, the Lord said, "Here's Emma." I'm not kidding. She floated a couple of inches off the floor. It was almost like Kathryn Kuhlman in those old videos when she wore a white dress and looked like she was gliding across the platform. Emma appeared beautiful and young - about 22 years old - but she was old at the same time. She seemed to carry the wisdom, virtue and grace of Proverbs 31 on her life. She glided into the room, emitting brilliant light and colors. Emma carried these bags and began pulling gold out of them. Then, as she walked up and down the aisles of the church, she began putting gold dust on people... Within three weeks of that visitation, the church had given me the biggest offering I had ever received to that point in my ministry. Thousands of dollars! Thousands! During this visitation the pastor's wife (it was an AOG church) got totally whacked by the Holy Ghost - she began running around barking like a dog or squawking like a chicken as a powerful prophetic spirit came on her. Also, as this prophetic anointing came on her, she started getting phone numbers of complete strangers and calling them up on the telephone and prophesying over them... Then angels started showing up in the church."[3]

This latest "revival" unfortunately, appears to be the next escalation of the part of the prophetic movement that has opened itself unchecked to new age techniques and teachings. I realize those not familiar with the prophetic movement will read the above and just think it is insanity. But I assure you – there *are* real supernatural manifestations going on in Florida and elsewhere as a result. These are all the more dangerous because they are real, and because the teachers are beginning to teach outright occult manifestations and experiences. God forbids us to talk to the dead. If Todd Bentley was not taken to heaven, and he was not talking with Paul, then he was speaking to a familiar spirit sent to lead him, and those who follow him, into gross spiritual darkness. Yes, people are getting healed at these meetings. God will always honor the faith of those who come to Him. But behind it all are teachings and experiences and manifestations that are virtually indistinguishable from what is seen, experienced, and taught in New Age centers worldwide. You cannot sanctify occult practices such as guided visualization, put Jesus' name on it and expect that God will be in it. People who say that Bentley and others may be off, yet are still insistent on having these kinds of experiences that come through these people, fail to understand that the Holy Spirit is *not* going to manifest himself through occult means or teachers of occult practices, and what they are getting is a counterfeit of the highest order.

As I was completing this writing, I was sent a very disturbing video over the internet. It was a promotional for a New Age healing practice called "Matrix Energetics." Its promoter is shown explaining how it works and clips from his seminars are shown, in which he is touching people and they are falling over, laughing hysterically, weeping for no reason, and talking about being healed.[4]

Exactly as it is taking place in Florida.

Except in Florida, the Name of Jesus is being used. Do we really have the discernment to know whether something is of God or not? I fear we are losing that most crucial weapon in our fight against deception in this last time.

We must do several things to keep ourselves from falling into the deception of false manifestations and miracles: Try the spirits, check the messengers out, and make sure everything is completely grounded in scripture, with no extra-scriptural, retranslated, or unscriptural teachings. Look for the fruit. Is it peaceable, orderly, full of love and grace, or is it chaotic, confusing, and uncontrolled?

We cannot shrink back from asking these questions. Too much is at stake. In this hour, the counterfeit, demonic miraculous is going to start appearing everywhere. More and more people are going to become demonized by the massive immersion in occult television shows, movies, music, and New Age teachings. God is going to need men and women of God like Daniel and his friends, who are able to stand in the midst of Babylon and *astound* and *confound* the "magick" or the magicians of this world with the true power of God - the true miraculous. It will not be parlor tricks, fake chicken feathers, dubious gemstones and embarrassing displays of childish emotional unrestraint, but the real miraculous that heals the sick, raises the dead and casts out devils. In the end the false miracles will be exposed before the witness to two true prophets who will call the *real* fire of God out of heaven in Jerusalem. Do not accept imitations. Test these things to the wall. God demands we do so or we will fall prey to some of the most head spinning supernatural manifestations hell has ever developed. Stand in the real. Do not be swayed by what you see. "Prove all things; hold fast that which is good." (1 Thessalonians 5:21) That is the command.

Chapter Seventeen

The Principle of Leaven

—⚏—

"A little leaven leaveneth the whole lump." (Galatians 5:9)

There is nowhere I have more clearly seen the danger of, and the results of, the leavening process as I have concerning the occult and New Age manifestations in the church in this generation. The scriptures are clear about not allowing sin or compromise to enter in: it is a cancer, a destructive and fast growing spirit killer. "Come out from among them, saith the Lord, and be ye separate, and touch not the unclean thing…" (2 Corinthians 6:17) God was very clear with Israel in these things: He warned them not to adopt any of the customs of the nations around them, especially the "abominable ones," lest the very land vomit them out. He was especially clear about adopting any occult practices: divination, necromancy, astrology, any supernatural workings outside the working of His mighty power by His Spirit. When Israel disobeyed and began adopting the customs of the surrounding nations, chaos and destruction followed.

Solomon had a shining career, a clear call and God-given gifts that made his time as King filled with glorious possibilities. But because of his weakness with women, he began to allow his many wives to bring in vile Pagan practices and god and goddess worship, and it completely unraveled the glory of his reign and began the beginning of the end for Israel as a united nation.

Compromise and adopting the world's ways always brings bad results. But there is one area that does more – opening the door to the occult and New Age practices. It opens the door to the super-natural. It opens the door to the demonic.

The standards of Christian conduct, so to speak, could not be clearer if you are a plain Bible reader. There are *very* few "gray areas." We've been able to see the ravaging effects of divorce, sexual promiscuity, pornography, and homosexuality on the church in the last few decades as we continue to lower the bar on what we deem acceptable. In fact, we keep changing the description of the bar. The result is that we have a Western church that is so weak that it cannot stand up to even the smallest of the devil's attacks. Satan just keeps pushing us back further and further and we keep letting him, until truly, as the Old Testament says, "There was no king over Israel, but every man did what was right in his own eyes." (Judges 21:25) The church is coming to that place. King Jesus is no longer ruling over the Western church, because everyone does what they think is right, interpreting, cutting out or changing the Bible to suit their own personal sin preferences, and we are the sad Emperor with no clothes, naked as a jaybird and acting like we're still something significant. We decry that we are socially irrelevant because *we are*. And the more we try, the more the world sees it for the fraud it is. The world doesn't need us to be relevant; why do we care what they want anyway? The world needs us to be Truth Bearers with the power of God to back up that truth, and the power to redeem through the plain proclamation of Jesus Christ and His sacrifice and resurrection.

But perhaps the worst compromise, the most deadly leaven and the final signal of the Apostasy is how we have swung wide the doors and let the occult powers come in. No, we don't have Ouija board Bible studies – yet. But I *did* see an "angel board" advertised, so you can "talk to your angels." I wonder how many Christians fell for that – and got demonized through it.

The Harry Potter debate was stunning to me. As a former occultist, the mere hint of witchcraft in any shape or form, real or fictional, was unacceptable and abhorrent. Why would anyone want to return to the garbage heap of demonic cesspools once they had tasted of the sweetness of the presence of the Holy Spirit? And yet,

I woke up one day having to speak to and address the Harry Potter madness – not just to educate believers in what we were facing – but shockingly, facing the fact that Christians themselves were falling for the Potter mania and they really, truly did not see anything wrong with it. When confronted, I got any number of excuses: It's just fantasy. It has good moral stories. It teaches kids to love reading. On it went. It became a completely frustrating and largely unsuccessful attempt to wake people up to the fact that the Potter Phenomenon was infecting people, and especially the church, with very dangerous occult imagery and imaginings.

Now, in retrospect, I realize Harry Potter was simply a very clever demonic plan to do three things: (1) Anesthetize an entire generation of children and young people to truth, (2) Destroy the "discernment gene" in the Body of Christ, and (3) Interest an entire generation of children in witchcraft and the occult. This is really important to me. All of what I have written in this book has been a cry for solid Biblical truth, watching the gates for deception, and for, true Biblical and spiritual discernment of truth from lie to be reestablished in the Body of Christ. I now realize that discernment has been fairly programmed *out* of the spiritual genetics of an entire generation of children, and that Christian children have grown up with the occult-vulnerable gene almost programmed *into* them instead. Once you accept the lie that the occult in any fashion, fiction or non-fiction, real or fantasy is acceptable, you have absolutely no protection against its eroding powers into the church, your family, your spiritual life.

I've seen the results of such erosion. As an example, a youth ministry I knew was doing a game imitating a popular TV show, and had the leaders dressed in loincloths with torches and war paint and standing at five points of the room, one for north, south, east and west, representing earth, air, fire and water, with someone in the middle, and not one leader had the discernment or knowledge that they were in fact setting the perfect stage for a pentacle-formed Wicca-type ceremony. Any Wiccan walking in off the streets would be perfectly at home and not even see the difference between Wicca and Christianity. Isn't that scary?

The erosion is seen in a Youth With A Mission Europe writer who wrote an article in October 2005 about attending an evangelism seminar where a speaker spoke of trying to reach the New Agers without "demonizing" them (I won't even go there) sharing his personal discovery of the "wisdom of the ages summarized and presented in pictorial form in the Tarot." The article went on to say that the message of the Tarot cards faces man's ultimate questions - who am I, why am I here, etc. - and leads ultimately to the key figure of the Fool, who has always been with us, calling us from death to new life, empowering us on the roller coaster of life. "The Tarot beyond prediction is a call to broaden our horizons beyond our consciousness, and to reconnect our souls with the divine source of all life," they concluded.

This is a perfect example of the insanity of the Emergent "incarnational mission" which is to "interact with the Pagan beliefs as they communicated the gospel." Of all the things I read in the Old Testament, sitting down and using Pagan occult rituals and rites to reach the Pagans is not in there. Nor is it in the New Testament, by the way. In the book of Acts, they *burned* their occult material. In the "incarnational mission," people *read up on it* so they can "reach" them. And thus we infect ourselves with information and literature that will open the door very wide to demonic influence in our own lives.

No one starts out intending to get deceived. People fall into deception for a number of reasons. But one thing they all have in common: they are not skilled in the Word of God. They do not know how to discern truth from error. They do not test the spirits. They are under the mistaken assumption that because a person is a nice and sincere person, what they teach must be okay, too…well, mostly okay. And that is the other problem with leaven: it's hard to see. Leaven is seen more in the way it manifests after the fact than when it first goes into the mix. Certain kinds of flour and yeast look somewhat similar if you are not watching your ingredient mixing closely. It only manifests after it is too late to remove the leaven without throwing out the whole loaf.

"Don't throw out the baby with the bathwater." This is one phrase right out of hell, right up there with "let's see what we *can* agree on." So many believers will give a pass to famous Christians who are beginning to teach error because, well, they're *famous*, and they wouldn't be famous if God hadn't blessed them, right? Actually, Satan too can promote someone who is unknowingly teaching lies and error if it suits him; it is still his world, after all. Oprah said she got down on her knees repeatedly and begged God to use her; she said the result is all the things she is now doing to promote New Age teachers like Marianne Williamson and Eckhart Tolle. Do you think it is God who blessed her? God is not the only one who answers prayer, friend. So yes, fame is irrelevant. If the teaching has become unscriptural and the teacher will not change or repent, then yes, you *do* reject it all. If you eat the bread and ignore the leaven, you will still be "leavened" by lies. No, we don't all hit the mark exactly. But the leaven that is coming in now is not just "well, they missed that one" but these teachers are producing a body of work and ministry that is riddled with the lies of eastern thought, dominionism, and other false teachings. "Don't throw out the baby with the bathwater." But this isn't *about* a baby. This is about occultic lies that threaten our children.

In the matter of occult teachings, there is no more serious matter in the church. It is the one thing that will certainly demonize those who open themselves to it. You cannot have a little Harry Potter in the church, or a few Yoga classes, or read an occasional zodiac prediction, or watch a few occult-tinged shows without it infecting your mind and heart, like spiritual pornography.

But when these occult teachings and practices come hidden in Christian disguises like "visualizing Jesus" or "breath prayers" or "Christian Yoga," we have opened ourselves to a world of hurt. There will be more to come: Earth worship and Wicca are reported is on the rise among evangelical youth, and there are even Christian Wiccan websites whose members see no contradiction between the Wiccan way and the Gospel of Jesus. The "synchronicity" that the FutureChurch has worked so diligently to produce between cultures and religions is now creating a Western Church that will soon be indistinguishable from any other religion, which will soon be absorbed into the One World Religion.

Chapter Eighteen

What Can We Do?

—ᗩᗯ—

Knowing that all these things have come, what are we as believers to do? We cannot and must not just throw in the towel and secede. No, there is too much at stake, especially for the next generation.

God has always had a remnant of truth-tellers and light bearers of Jesus. We must do all we can to prepare this generation – which could be the *last* generation – to do battle against the lies of Lucifer and the spirit of this age. Here is what we must do:

1. Return to teaching and preaching the pure Word of God, especially to youth. We can no longer afford to consider youth ministry as professional babysitting and entertainment. We need fewer "youth directors" and more "youth pastors" who are not just hired hands looking for a higher paying job as a "real" pastor, but those who understand the gravity of caring for young lambs and are willing to invest the prayer, energy and teaching necessary to raise them to be solid believers and tested warriors. They must be willing to divest their ministries of cute psychological programs and return to hard-core tackling of real life issues with the powerful Word of Truth.

2. Stop worrying about "relevance." The world could care less if we are relevant. They need to know that we are *real*, and the fact is, the truth is *always* relevant. The more you dress

the truth in the modern monkey suit of the cultural moment, the less power it has to help –or save – anyone at all.

3. Divest yourselves of everything and anything related to the occult and the New Age – television shows, movies, comics, video games, books, music, anything with even a HINT of occult or New Age content. You will never have clear discernment if your vision is clouded by even a hint of these things. You cannot do spiritual warfare against the enemy if you have his toys in your private collection.

4. Get your church off the squirrel cage of the Purpose-Driven model. Satan drives. The Spirit of God leads. I have seen enough of the purpose-driven, megachurch model to know that for every sliver of real ministry that happens, it has to go through reams of papers, meetings and corporate decisions. How much more could we do if we simply started being the church, instead of coming up with every trick in the book to "make growth happen?" The true church growth plan is simple, and powerful: "And the Lord added to the church daily such as should be saved." (Acts 2:47)

5. Make a decision to teach – and learn – spiritual warfare. The scriptures are clear that we are not to be ignorant of Satan's devices, and right now, the church is as ignorant as it can possibly be. We simply must begin to teach people how to fight the good fight and do hand to hand combat with the enemy for the souls of those who are lost. We must teach how to live godly lives that will prevent Satan from gaining a stronghold in us, and if he has it, how to break it in real deliverance prayer.

6. Begin to teach once more the reality of the prophetic and the scriptures old and new concerning the return of Jesus Christ, the coming deception, the signs to look for, and how to prepare ourselves, whether he comes next year, tomorrow, or a decade from now. We cannot afford to leave the church unprepared for what is sure to come.

7. Divest ourselves of silly, trivial, shallow, pseudo-deep, socialist imitations of Gospel books and media. Begin to read and stock up on proven classics, i.e., My Utmost for His

Highest, A.W. Tozer, Amy Carmichael, etc. In the glaring absence of much of anything with any substance in our current FutureChurch, it may just inspire someone to begin writing books and study materials of depth and value – the kind that only come from wrestling with God and living a committed life to Jesus Christ.

8. Ask God to give you true discernment, and be willing to act on what He shows you.

9. Make the altar and prayer the center of our church once more. For every moment of preaching or teaching, we ought to be spending at least that much time on our knees. What we lack – have lacked for some time, which is how we got to this place – is the understanding that the power of the Gospel is rooted in true, committed intercessory prayer. Without that, we simple devolve into the mess we have become – a shell of a church that is propped up by programs, fed by the culture, promoted by worldly schemes, and powered by human will. God deliver us from that through a revival of true fiery prayer and intercession in this hour.

10. We must prepare for persecution. Those who are determined to stay true to the Word of God and to walk in the power of God as they did in the book of Acts are going to face a time – soon – when they will be forced to pay a price for their faith that will not just be ridicule and criticism, ostracizing and isolation, but legal persecution, and before it is over, criminal prosecution and eventual martyrdom. Fear none of these things – but learn to prepare by making Jesus Christ the absolute center of your life, and the Word of God your sword, shield and unchangeable truth.

The next few years are going to be crucial to both the formation of the FutureChurch and the raising up of a generation to withstand the wave of deception, debilitation, disempowerment and darkness that is going to overwhelm the modern church. My prayer is that something shared in this book has moved you to resist being part of this FutureChurch, no matter how much you are isolated, mocked, pressured and ridiculed for taking a stand, and that you become part of God's last battalion of truth bearers and truth tellers before He comes. As we used to say in the early days, Maranatha! The Lord Comes!

YouthFire
www.gregoryreid.com
Box 370006
El Paso, TX 79037

Recommended Reading

—ɯ—

The Beautiful Side of Evil
by Johanna Michaelson, Harvest House, Eugene, Oregon, 1982

Like Lambs To The Slaughter
By Johanna Michealsen, Harvest House, Eugene, Oregon, 1989

The Hidden Dangers of the Rainbow
by Constance Cumbey, Huntington House, Shreveport, Louisiana,
1983

*Deceived On Purpose: The New Age Implications of the
Purpose-Driven Church*
by Warren Smith, Mountain Stream Press, Magalia, California,
2004

Reinventing Jesus Christ
by Warren Smith, Conscience Press, Ravenna, Ohio, 2002
www.reinventingjesuschrist.com

The Light That Was Dark
by Warren Smith, Lighthouse Trails Publishing, Salem, Oregon,
2005

A Time of Departing
by Ray Yungen, Lighthouse Trails Publishing, Salem, Oregon,
2006

For Many Shall Come In My Name
by Ray Yungen, Lighthouse Trails Publishing, Salem, Oregon, 2007

Faith Undone
By Roger Oakland, Lighthouse Trails Publishing, Salem, Oregon, 2007

Devil Take the Youngest
By Winkie Pratney, Huntington House, Shreveport, Louisiana, 1985

The Dark Side of the Purpose Driven Church Expanded Edition
By Noah W. Hutchings, Bible Belt Publishing, Bethany, Oklahoma, 2007

Endnotes

—៣—

Everything Will Change

1. Barbara Marx Hubbard, *Happy Birth Day, Planet Earth*
2. Rick Warren, Pastors.Com, Ministry Toolbox, 6/14/2006
3. Leonard Sweet, Emergent Church leader, *Soul Tsunami*, Pp. 17, 75
4. Eckhart Tolle, New Age writer, *A New Earth*, Pp. 21-22

Chapter One – Once Upon A Time
1. Neale Donald Walsch, *Conversations with God: an uncommon dialogue, Book 2* (Charlottesville, Virginia: Hampton Roads Publishing Company, Inc., 1997) p. 35
2. Ibid., p. 55
3. Ibid., p. 42
4. http://www.crossroad.to/charts/millennium-goals-peace.htm
5. Rick Warren, May 23, 2005, Pew Forum on Religion: http://pewforum.org/events/index.php?EventID=80

Chapter Two – The Occult, The New Age and The Emergent Church: Understanding The Basics
1. http://www.lausanne.org/lausanne-1974/lausanne-covenant.html
   http://www.crossroad.to/articles2/006/dwayna/emnr.htm

Chapter Three – First Lessons In Discernment
1. William P. Young *The Shack* (Windblown Media Los Angeles, California, 2007), p. 208)

Chapter Five - The FutureYouth: Defining "Christian" for the Next Generation
1. Dan Kimball, *They Like Jesus but Not the Church: Insights from Emerging Generations*, (Zondervan, Grand Rapids Michigan, 2007)

Chapter Eight – East Meets West: Contemplative Prayer, Christian Yoga and Spiritual Deformation
1. Harold Balyoz, *Three Remarkable Women* (Atlas Publishers, Flagstaff, Arizona,1986) p. 195
2. Barbara Marx Hubbard, *The Revelation: A Message of Hope for the New Milennium (Nataraj Publishing, Novato, California* (1993,1995) p. 55
3. Ibid., p. 76
4. http://www.abraham-hicks.com/lawofattractionsource/mp3downloads.php
5. **http://blogs.echurchnetwork.net/Newsletter/perma-link/00003.aspx)**
6. Yoga Journal, May/June 1993, p. 69
7. David Steindl-Rast, "Recollection of Thomas Merton's Last Days in the West" (Monastic Studies, 7:10, 1969).
8. From *Sabbatical Journey*, Henri Nouwen's last book, p. 51, 1998 Hardcover edition

Chapter Nine – Velvet Elvis or False Jesus?
1. *The Emergent Mystique* by Andy Crouch, Christianity Today, November 1, 2004
2. http://blogs.echurchnetwork.net/Assets/UserBlog/314/052905.mp3
3. Ibid.
4. E-mail, sent 11/15/2006
5. E-mail received 11/16/2006
6. E-mail sent 11/16/2006

7. E-mail received 11/16/2006
8. E-mail sent 11/16/2006
9. E-mail received 11/16/2006
10. *The God We Never Knew: Beyond Dogmatic Religion To A More Authentic Contemporary Faith*, Marcus J Borg, Harper One, May 6, 1998
11. Ibid., p. 25
12. *Final Preparations to Receive the New Age Christ* by Prof. Johan Malan, Middelburg, South Africa, March 12, 2008, www.bibleguidance.co.za
13. *The God We Never Knew*, p. 25
14. From *Christianity Today* interview, "The Emergent Mystique," Sept. 7th, 2007.
15. *The God We Never Knew.* p.20
16. From Mars Hill Website, *Our Shared Values [Directions,]* http://www.marshill.org/believe/directions/ and *Mars Hill Narrative Theology*, http://www.marshill.org/believe/
17. *Velvet Elvis:Repainting the Christian Faith,* Rob Bell, (Zondervan, Grand Rapids Michigan, 2005) p. 26
18. *Velvet Elvis,* p. 192
19. Roger Oakland, *Faith Undone*, (Salem, Oregon, Lighthouse Trails Publishing, 2007) p.110
20. *Velvet Elvis,* p.11
21. Ibid., p. 21
22. Ibid.
23. Ibid.
24. Ibid.
25. Ibid., p.23
26. Ibid.
27. Ibid, pp. 26-27
28. Ibid., p. 27
29. Ibid.
30. Ibid., p. 28
31. Ibid., p.50
32. Ibid., p. 53
33. Ibid., p. 62
34. Ibid.

35. Ibid., p. 51
36. Ibid., p.67
37. Ibid., p. 68
38. Ibid., p. 83
39. Ibid. p. 118
40. Ibid., p. 133
41. *A Return To Love: Reflections on the Principles of A Course in Miracles,* (Harper Collins Publishers, New York, New York, 1992) Chapter 7, Section 3, Pg. 190-191.
42. *Velvet Elvis,* p. 134
43. Ibid., p. 142
44. Ibid.
45. Ibid., p. 148
46. Ibid., p. 150
47. Ibid., p.158
48. (http://www.seedsofcompassion.org/involved/interreligious_day.asp)

Chapter Ten – Heaven On Earth
1. Barbara Marx Hubbard, *The Revelation: A Message of Hope for the New Milennium* (Nataraj Publishing, Novato, California (1993,1995) p. 74
2. Ibid., p. 85
3. Alice Bailey, *From Bethlehem to Calvary,* Chapter Five – The Fourth Initiation, the Crucifixion
4. Brian McLaren, *The Secret Message of Jesus,* (W Publishing Group A Division of Thomas Nelson, Inc., Nashville, Tennessee, 2006) p. 23
5. Rick Warren, *The Purpose-Driven Life: What On Earth Am I Here For?,* (Zondervan, Grand Rapids Michigan, 2002) p. 285
6. http://www.wecansolveit.org/pages/partners/
7. http://www.earthday.net/
8. http://www.earthday.net/~earthday/node/73
9. Ibid.

10. http://salsa.democracyinaction.org/o/1807/t/5340/signUp.jsp?key=2184&t=ProgramsEventsTemplate.dwt&Country=US
11. http://www.globalsecurity.org/wmd/library/news/iran/2007/iran-070926-irna01.htm

Chapter Eleven – The Problem With Rick Warren
1. http://www.time.com/time/covers/1101050207/photoessay/
2. http://encarta.msn.com/encyclopedia_761561733/billy_graham.html
3. http://www.christianitytoday.com/ct/2002/november18/1.42.html?start=3
4. http://www.crossroad.to/Quotes/spirituality/peale.htm
5. http://www.rapidnet.com/~jbeard/bdm/exposes/schuller/general.htmhttp://www.reinventingjesuschrist.com/updates/1.html
6. http://www.worldnetdaily.com/index.php?fa=PAGE.view&pageId=38958
7. Rick Warren's Ministry Toolbox, Issue #321, 7/25/2007

Chapter Twelve – Where Did The Devil Go?
1. Brian McLaren, *The Secret Message of Jesus,* (W Publishing Group A Division of Thomas Nelson, Inc., Nashville, Tennessee, 2006) pp. 63-64
2. Eckhart Tolle, *A New Earth: Awakening to Your Life's Purpose,* (Dutton Adult, Penguin Group, New York, New York, 2005) p.1
3. http://www.bpnews.net/bpnews.asp?id=27867
4. Ibid.
5. http://en.wikipedia.org/wiki/James_Pike
6. Winkie Pratney, *Devil Take the Youngest*, (Lafayette, Louisiana: Huntington House, 1985)

Chapter Thirteen – The Battle for the Bible – Get the Message?
1. http://www.jesus-is-lord.com/hort.htm   http://www.historicist.com/necromancers/nabv30gguild.htm

2. Rick Warren, *The Purpose-Driven Church: Growth Without Compromising Your Message & Mission*, (Grand Rapids, Michigan: Zondervan, 1995, p.297

3. *A Course In Miracles,* (Foundation for Inner Peace, Mill Valley, California)

4. Marianne Williamson, *A Return to Love: Reflections on the Principles of "A Course in Miracles"*, (HarperCollins Publishers, New York, NY, 1996)

5. Warren Smith, *The Light That Was Dark,* (Lighthouse Trails Publishing, Salem, Oregon, 1995)

6. Warren Smith, *Deceived On Purpose: The New Age Implications of the Purpose Driven Church,* (Mountain Stream Press, Magalia, California, 2004)

7. http://www.themystica.org/mystica/articles/a/below_above.html

8. William P. Young, *The Shack*, (Windblown Media, Los Angeles California) 1997

9. Ibid., Front Cover endorsement

10. http://www.northernway.org/sophia.html

11. June 29, 2004, World Net Daily.

12. http://www.worldnetdaily.com/index.php?fa=PAGE.view&pageId=25310

Chapter Sixteen – Signs and Wonders

1. http://www.saibabamiracles.com/baba/index.html

2. From "A False Healing Revival?" e-mail alert from Revival List, April 23, 2008.

3. http://www.etpv.org/2003/angho.html

4. http://www.youtube.com/watch?v=6h0ZRFPfxSs

Printed in the United States
130308LV00006B/121/P